CREATING A MILLION-DOLLAR-A-YEAR SALES INCOME

Paul M. McCord

John Wiley & Sons, Inc.

Published by John Wiley & Sons, Inc., Hoboken, New Jersey.
Published simultaneously in Canada.

Library of Congress Cataloging-in-Publication Data:

McCord, Paul.
  Creating a million-dollar-a-year sales income : sales success through client referrals / Paul McCord
      p. cm.
  Includes index
  ISBN-13: 978-0-470-04549-7 (pbk. : alk. paper)
  ISBN-10: 0-470-04549-3 (pbk. : alk. paper)
  1. Selling. 2. Business referrals. I. Title.

  HF5438.25.M3956 2007
  658.85—dc22

2006011010

Printed in the United States of America.
10 9 8 7 6 5 4 3 2 1

This book is dedicated to my wife Debbie, whose encouragement and support have been a Godsend, and to all of my former managers, mentors, and trainers who so graciously imparted their knowledge and experience to me.

ABOUT THE AUTHOR

Paul has had a distinguished career in teaching, sales, sales training, and sales management. A magna cum laude graduate of Texas A&M University, Commerce, with graduate studies at Texas Christian University in Ft. Worth, Paul began his career teaching literature at his alma mater. Although he enjoyed the challenges of teaching, his competitive nature lead him into the business world, where he could more fully utilize his selling and training talents.

Over the past two decades, Paul has excelled as salesman, trainer, and manager in the financial services industry. He has developed and lead sales teams wholesaling investment products to banks, credit unions, NASD broker/dealer firms, financial planning firms, trust companies, and major warehouse companies; operated his own successful mortgage company; and recruited, trained, and lead sales forces for several mortgage banks. He has had the pleasure of training thousands of salespeople and managers from almost any industry one can think of, but all have one thing in common—a desire to become the best sales person in their company.

Like most executives, Paul quickly realized the key to a successful company was the sales force. Throughout his career, Paul has studied the major issues facing the sales team: which candidates have the makeup to succeed? What training actually works? What recruiting methods produce effective, long-term results? How do you best coach and mentor professional salespeople? What are the key indicators of short-term and long-term success? Why do some sales plans work and others that appear to be just as viable, fall flat?

Paul has developed some effective, exciting solutions to several of these vexing issues. In addition, Paul works with companies to analyze and fix their issues in finding, attracting, and retaining top people, developing sales plans that work, and performing crisis analysis to determine where the weaknesses are and how to turn them into strengths.

Paul may be reached at pmccord@mccordandassociates.com, or through his web sites: http://www.mccordandassociates.com, his company website with extensive information on his sales training and management consulting experience and capabilities; http://www.businessresearchdatabase.com, a free site he established to provide salespeople, professionals, and companies with free tools to research prospects, competitors, and industries, as well as to perform in-depth economic, demographic, and marketing research; and http://www.pwwrselling.com, the companion site to this book.

CONTENTS

INTRODUCTION

*C*reating a Million-Dollar-a-Year Sales Income is the culmination of 20 years of formal and informal research into selling. During my career I've had the opportunity to sell millwork, wholesale investments to NASD broker/dealers, retail mortgages, and offer sales training and management consulting to companies of all types and sizes. Although most of my selling experience is business-to-business, I've spent several years selling financial products directly to consumers.

Like most salespeople, I've experimented with different techniques, investigated sales theories, attended countless seminars, read hundreds of books, and—after I began training salespeople over 14 years ago—closely observed what appeared to work (or didn't work) for other salespeople.

For many years I used tried and true methods from other sales trainers and successful salespeople who were kind enough to enlighten the rest of us by distilling their experience and knowledge into books, classes, and seminars. Most of that information focused on specific parts of the selling process—prospecting, marketing, presentations, trial closes, and the like. After a while, I realized one particular area wasn't addressed often or well enough: how to generate referrals from clients and prospects.

INTRODUCTION

Almost without fail, sales trainers and top salespeople stressed the need for salespeople to work from referrals, claiming that referrals lower the cost of sales and increase sales income. But no one told us *how* we could actually generate these referrals. Advice was limited to asking the customer for referrals after completing a sale. Once in a while I found a few specific details, such as having the customer write a referral letter or asking the client to call a prospect and introduce the salesperson over the phone. Great suggestions, but this advice didn't answer the basic question: How can we get our clients to give referrals in the first place?

As my sales and sales training career progressed, I talked to successful salespeople and experimented with various methods for generating referrals. I compiled the information, refined it, and created the PWWR (pronounced *Power*) Referral Generation System to generate the type and volume of referrals I wanted. The PWWR system addresses and eliminates problems and issues that have historically kept salespeople from generating large numbers of quality referrals. The system uses a simple but comprehensive system of Planting referral seeds, Watering them during the course of the sale, Weeding out problems and objections, and Reaping the rewards: a large number of high quality referrals.

Referral Generation Tip

Using the PWWR system during the course of your sale is simple: just remember to Plant the seeds, Water them throughout the sale, Weed out any issues, and Reap the referrals. It's PWWR!

2

I soon began teaching the PWWR Referral Generation System to other salespeople. Based on their reactions and results, I fine-tuned the system and developed reliable, flexible techniques that can be used and replicated by any salesperson. The training sessions eventually became an all-day training seminar. This book evolved from that background.

Most of the statistical information in this book comes directly from attendees of my training seminars. I used them as laboratory participants to refine my methods and help me understand why salespeople have problems generating referrals, and how they can use the methods I teach.

I don't know of any "official" statistics documenting the generation of referrals, the closing ratio of sales from referrals, or the increase of sales volume due to referrals. I obtained the information within this book from salespeople and managers in my seminars, and from successful salespeople in many industries. Surprisingly, much of what I discovered meshes with the conclusions of others who've informally studied this issue. For instance, less than 15% of my attendees generate enough referrals to significantly impact their sales volume (defining significant impact as generating at least 20% of their sales from referrals). Other sales trainers who've studied the issue claim this number is less than 10%. Although our percentages differ, we agree that only a small number of salespeople generate adequate referrals.

Although I've gathered statistics from my seminars and am confident of the numbers presented here, I don't want to give the impression the statistics were generated by a formal academic study. Nor do I claim any of the methods are original or unique. I've spoken to hundreds of salespeople who already use various combinations of the techniques presented here. My contribution is collecting these tools and molding them into a cohesive referral generation program that can be adapted to virtually any sales method. These are simply the tools and techniques the Million-Dollar-a-Year sales superstars use, implemented into a systematic program.

HOW TO USE THE INFORMATION

I hope each of you will think about your personal needs as you read this book. Absorb the information and mold it to fit your circumstances and personality. Most of the techniques can be used independently of each other. Some salespeople will use every method presented here, while others may feel intimidated by the need to ask each client for at least five quality referrals. Still others may not have the confidence to ask for referral lunches with prospects. But even the newest salesperson can begin using some of these techniques right away. And certainly, not every Million-Dollar-a-Year megaproducer uses each and every technique. Each megaproducer has integrated into his or her selling system the techniques that he or she feels comfortable with.

The more of these you incorporate into your sales calls, the better the results you'll achieve. Some techniques require a fair amount of practice; others are probably extensions and refinements of techniques you currently use. The key is to become totally comfortable with each concept before introducing it to a client. Then integrate the referral system into your selling model so it becomes a natural part of how you sell.

DEVELOPING YOUR REFERRAL GENERATION SKILLS

Throughout this book, I'll encourage you to visit the PWWR Referral Generation System web site (www.pwwrreferrals.com) for examples of successful ways to overcome objections and answer prospect questions. The web site features a discussion board where you can exchange tips with other sales professionals and seek (or give) advice. You'll also find extensive lists of organizations, materials, and web sites to help research potential prospects, a database of articles on various aspects of selling, and other information designed to help salespeople generate sales, refine their selling methods, and increase their sales volume. The web site is divided into a free section and a coaching section. As you work on developing new approaches, you'll find encouragement and support online. I update the web site on a regular basis with articles, tips, and contributions from other salespeople who discuss their successes—and their failures. I hope you'll soon write your own success story!

CHAPTER

Why
Salespeople
Fail

One of the questions I hear most often from corporate executives and salespeople is, "Why do salespeople fail?" Generally speaking, salespeople fail because they lack desire, commitment, selling skills, and/or training.

LACK OF DESIRE

A strong desire to succeed is a prerequisite for success in sales. Professional selling is a tough occupation. On most days, a salesperson will hear the word *no* more often than *yes*. At the beginning of a sales career or when changing jobs, each salesperson spends a huge amount of time prospecting for leads. In spite of the hard work that's required up front, sales can also be a tremendously rewarding and lucrative career—if you begin with a sincere, heartfelt desire to succeed. You must have a passion to make those sales. This desire can't be faked, but it *can* be fed. If the initial spark is present, training and encouragement will help it grow.

Many of us enjoy certain aspects of sales: signing a contract with a tough client; the completion of a long-term sale; earning a good commission; and having a significant amount of freedom and control over how we spend our time. On the flip side, salespeople work long hours with no guaranteed income and face rejection, competition, stress, sales quotas, and many other issues on a daily basis.

Desire is the *need* to accomplish the goal of selling a product or service. One of the definitions of desire is "the feeling that accompanies an unsatisfied state." Without the accomplishments of selling, the salesperson feels unfulfilled. The successful salesperson has an emotional need to be fed the fruits of sales success.

LACK OF COMMITMENT

Unfortunately, desire alone doesn't ensure success. I've talked with many former salespeople who wanted to succeed, viewed sales as a noble and honorable profession, and had a strong desire to make a significant income. Yet they failed because they lacked commitment. They weren't willing to take the punishment of being rejected more often than not; they weren't willing to put in the time required; they weren't willing to invest in themselves and learn the profession; and they weren't willing to take the advice, constructive criticism, and guidance of their peers, managers, and prospects who chose not to purchase.

Desire is the *want* or *need to succeed,* while commitment is the *determination* and *willingness to do whatever is needed* to achieve success. Selling is a demanding occupation. Most professional sales positions require more than 40 hours per week. Generally, a salesperson can expect to work longer and harder than anyone else in his or her company. Clients don't necessarily need you when it's convenient—they need you when they need you. And that can be any time—day, night, weekends, holidays, or during your vacation.

As previously mentioned, selling requires the commitment to work through a number of activities most salespeople find difficult and even distasteful. The sales process must begin with a prospect to sell to—and prospecting is the single biggest commitment killer in sales. More than any other factor, lack of commitment to work through the initial failure and frustration of prospecting drives people out of sales. Although it's a cliché, the sales profession truly is a numbers game, and the successful salesperson needs to keep a constant flow of prospects in the pipeline. Most people who don't make it in sales fail because they lack the commitment and persistence to consistently initiate the beginning of the sales process—finding someone to sell to.

Salespeople have a number of prospecting methods at their disposal—cold-calling; buying and working leads; paying for mass direct-marketing campaigns; purchased advertising; networking; and, for a few, generating referrals from existing clients and prospects.

Cold-calling is a time-honored method, and also the most difficult form of prospecting. Picking up a phone and calling a complete stranger who will most likely say "no" is the most terrifying and discouraging part of selling. And we get to do it over and over, every day, until we build our businesses. Whether the sales are business-to-

Referral Generation Tip

Price Doesn't Have to Be King: If price is a hindrance to your selling success, you must begin to develop a large number of quality referrals. Referral selling is the only consistent prospecting method that eliminates price as a primary factor in the sale.

business or direct to the public, cold-calling flushes more people from the ranks of sales than any other single aspect of the profession.

Close behind cold-calling is working sales leads. Despite what most lead supply companies claim, sales leads are virtually the same as cold-calling, even though the prospect indicated some level of interest in the product. Unfortunately, other salespeople have already contacted many of these leads. Purchasing leads means you've taken one step forward in prospecting—you have reason to believe the person is interested in your product or service. You've also taken two steps back, because you know competitors will also come calling—and that will probably create a price issue.

Most new salespeople can't afford to create a marketing campaign through media advertising or direct mail. In a major market, a small newspaper display advertisement may cost well over a thousand dollars. Direct mail usually costs at least seventy-five cents per piece. Both marketing methods require long-term exposure to generate results. Consequently, the average salesperson would spend thousands of dollars before generating a single prospect—tens of thousands before generating enough prospects to stay in business.

Another common prospecting method is networking through members of organizations, family, friends, and acquaintances. In many cases, this is where the salesperson finds his or her early customers and clients. It's a perfect place to start, but that's exactly what it is—a beginning. Most of us don't have enough contacts to generate major sales activity, although these early leads may sustain our businesses for a month or two. When your family and friends go into hiding, it's time to develop new leads!

A few salespeople are lucky enough to have their companies purchase leads, advertise, send out direct mail campaigns, and sell products and services, providing the salesperson with a few walk-ins or call-ins. But even these setups have serious limitations. Leads purchased by companies are usually the same leads a salesperson would purchase him- or herself, and the company divides these leads among a number of salespeople. Even industries usually considered to be "walk-in," such as furniture stores and automobile sales, tell new salespeople up front, "If you want to make money you can't rely on walk-ins alone."

Other prospecting methods include trade shows, seminars, and conventions. These prospecting methods have the same problems and limitations as those outlined previously, and may require a fair amount of experience, sophistication, and expense on the part of the salesperson or company.

The sad fact is, over 85% of professional salespeople rely on one or more of these prospecting methods outlined for virtually all of their prospect-generating activity. In my referral selling seminars, I ask attendees to list their top five prospecting methods in descending order, from most productive to least productive. When the lists are ready, I ask them to write every sale they made in the past year and which method generated that prospect. Almost without fail, an amazing thing happens. When we read these initial prospecting method lists, nearly everyone in the room has placed referrals in position number two. In other words, my seminar attendees claim referrals are the second-best method they have for generating sales. But when they do the actual list of sales and what method generated that sale, referrals turn up in last place—if they make the list at all. I find a serious reality gap between how salespeople *believe* they obtain sales and how they *really* generate new sales.

Why the disconnect? Since every person is told within five minutes of entering a professional selling position that in order to stay in business he or she needs to generate referrals, and since sales managers expect salespeople to have referrals, and since most salespeople ask for the occasional referral and often get a name and a phone number or two, salespeople believe they're selling by referral. They believe because they're getting names and phone numbers, they must be getting referral business. Only when they actually see where their business is coming from do most recognize how little business they generate from referrals. Certainly, many get a referral sale or two here and there, but not nearly as many as they feel they're generating.

With over 85% of professional salespeople forced to dig on a daily basis for prospects to fill their pipeline, is it any wonder so many good people fail? Desire can only go so far. Commitment isn't easy to maintain when we face a lifetime of turning over every rock in the field to find a prospect. Most of us can only hear *no* so many times before our enthusiasm wanes and our prospecting activity slows to an eventual halt. And at that point, whether we recognize it at the time or not, we are out of business.

LACK OF A GOOD SELLING PROCESS

Strong desire and commitment won't prevent failure unless they're accompanied by a proven way to generate prospects and close business deals. The second most frustrating thing for salespeople is the feeling of being lost in the sales event itself. Most companies, from mom-and-pop firms to Fortune 100 companies, do a good job of training their sales force on product, but they do a poor job when it comes to teaching the sales force *how to sell.* The two issues aren't the same, although many companies treat them as such.

Selling is the *how* in the sales process—how to get in front of and sell a prospect. Product knowledge is the *why*—why we sell and why the customer buys. Every salesperson needs solid grounding in both of these areas. Companies tend to view the why of selling as the crucial area, and to a certain extent they're right. Selling skills are transferable from company to company, industry to industry. Product knowledge is usually specific to an industry and a particular company within that industry. Consequently, the product and how to sell that particular product tops the training list for most firms.

But every salesperson needs a process to generate a robust pipeline of prospects and turn those prospects into customers. That proven process should include a prospecting method, a sales method, and a follow-up method that consistently generates fresh prospects. These prospects are converted into customers who receive a purchasing experience beyond their expectations.

15

A proven, reliable sales process will give you the confidence to tackle the most difficult client or the most demanding sales manager.

LACK OF TRAINING

Although desire and commitment are internally generated, a good selling process comes from training, and then adapting that training to your personality through trial and error. Lack of training is second only to a lack of commitment in flushing salespeople out of the business. Sales training is the foundation upon which product training should rest. Many companies assume their salespeople and the salespeople they hire already have a solid foundation in sales training. Salespeople who don't perform are simply written off as part of the 80% in the old 80/20 rule of selling: 80% of the sales force produces only 20% of the company's sales. Or, put another way, 80% of the company's sales are produced by only 20% of the sales force.

Studies show the top salespeople in any industry produce almost four times the sales volume of the average salesperson and 10 times the volume of the bottom dwellers. A survey of the top salespeople in your company would probably reveal a common denominator. All of them either received serious, in-depth sales training early in their careers through their company, or they've heavily invested in themselves by reading sales books, attending seminars, listening to sales tapes, and discussing with one another what works and what doesn't. Virtually every top salesperson spends a significant amount of time and money on personal training.

This doesn't let your company off the hook. Your employer should hire outside trainers to hold on-site seminars; top producers within

16

the company should hold training sessions; and the company should send its sales force to seminars. You and the other salespeople in your company should insist on being correctly trained.

Furthermore, it's in the company's best interest to spend dollars and time to train its salespeople. Is it any surprise that most of the top talent work for, or came from, companies that spend a tremendous amount of money on sales and product training?

Whether you're beginning a sales career, haven't received sufficient training in the past, or you're a well-trained, seasoned professional, every salesperson needs continual updates on both sales and product. If your company doesn't provide sufficient training (and most do not), you can invest in yourself by reading the best books on selling, attending sales seminars, using audiotapes and CDs, hiring a sales coach from one of the hundreds of sales training companies, and acquiring a mentor.

No salesperson ever reaches the point where he or she no longer needs training. Every top-producing salesperson I've met takes this aspect of the job seriously and spends a great deal of time on personal training. On the other hand, inexperienced salespeople often use lack of training as an excuse to not sell: "I can't go out there yet—I'm not ready!"

On-the-job training makes it perfectly acceptable to begin selling *before* you have complete knowledge of the product or service. New salespeople can sell most products and services with only a basic amount of training. You don't need to have the answer for every possible question. Don't hide behind training because you're afraid of failure, and don't let training become a stumbling block that keeps you from doing your job.

Sales failure is actually an important training tool. In fact, we probably learn more from failure than we learn from success. Even experienced salespeople fail. But fear of failure, which afflicts the salesperson who insists on complete training before entering the battlefield, is a self-fulfilling prophecy that guarantees failure through lack of activity.

For more information on how to handle rejection as you develop a referral business, how to find and hire a coach, and where to find additional sales training, go to the PWWR Referral Generation System web site: www.pwwrreferrals.com. For a discounted fee, you can take a professional sales assessment developed by Profiles International, one of the leading sales assessment companies in the world. Simply click on the "Sales Assessment" link. The results of this assessment will provide an overview of your selling strengths and weaknesses, plus solid suggestions you can use for self-coaching or in conjunction with a personal coach or mentor.

TAKING INVENTORY

Before we discuss how to develop a referral-generating relationship with your customers, let's take inventory of where you stand in each of the four areas discussed so far. Please write your answers to the following questions in the spaces provided.

Desire:

Do you have a burning desire to succeed in sales?

_____

If you could enter any field and do anything you wanted for a living, what would it be?

_____

_____

If selling isn't a key part of your previous answer, why?

_____

_____

Are you making the income you desire?

_____

Are you making the income you envisioned when you entered sales?

_____

Commitment:

If you do have the desire to succeed in sales, do you also have the commitment?

_____

Do you have the mental and emotional toughness to continue, despite setbacks and disappointments?

_____

How do you handle the frustration and feelings of failure brought on by being told "no"?

_____

_____

_____

_____

_____

The Process:

Do you have a proven, reliable selling process that takes you from prospecting to the final aspects of customer service? Can this process be replicated time after time?

_____

_____

What are your primary methods for generating new prospects?

_____

_____

_____

Do you have a plan for moving your business to a new level?

_____

Training:

Have you been thoroughly trained in selling (not product)?

_____

How many hours per year do you invest in your career through reading, company training, attending seminars, listening to tapes, being mentored or coached, and analyzing what works and doesn't work in your sales process?

_____

What sales books, by title, have you read in the last year?

_____

_____

_____

_____

What seminars have you attended?

_____

_____

_____

_____

What tapes have you listened to?

_____

_____

_____

_____

Have you hired a coach?

_____

What steps are you willing to take to improve your sales performance?

_____

_____

CHAPTER

Referrals
Are the
Solution

Referral selling is the solution to many of the problems discussed in Chapter 1. Although referrals won't give you the desire to succeed, they can feed that desire. Although they cannot give you the commitment for success, they can drive that commitment forward. Referrals are a vital part of a good sales process, and you *can* learn to generate them.

WHAT IS A REFERRAL?

First we need to be clear as to what a referral is and what it isn't. Many salespeople believe the name and phone number of a person or business given to you by a prospect or a customer constitutes a referral. A name and phone number are not a referral—they are a name and phone number, period.

Let's go back a couple of steps and define what a prospect is. The purpose of prospecting is to find an entity—an individual or a business—with a need for and the ability to acquire your product or service. We can divide individuals and businesses into four groups, and each group gets us closer to the sale.

The first group includes all the people and businesses in existence. No matter what product or service we sell, we begin our prospecting activity with this group of entities as potential customers. However, we need to divide this huge number into something more manageable. Applying a few basic criteria will eliminate most of these entities: age, geographic location, business type, income bracket, company size, and so on.

This gives us a much smaller group of people or businesses who may be likely suspects for our product or service. And that's exactly

Referral Generation Tip

Know Whom to Prospect: Analyze your last 100 customers. Can you find any patterns that can help you pinpoint your ideal prospect? If 73 of your last 100 clients were middle-aged men suffering from male pattern baldness, is this by accident or is this group the market you relate to best? If you find patterns, try to analyze why they exist. If you determine these patterns indicate which group or groups you best relate to, use that information and target your marketing to individuals in these groups.

what these folks are—*suspects*. We suspect they might be able to use what we're selling. So far, they seem to match the criteria we've developed.

The next step is to determine whether these suspects are true prospects; that is, whether they actually *can* use our product. We do this in a number of ways, such as talking directly to the suspects or doing background research. In the end, we must answer the central question: Do they have a need for our product/service or will our product/service meet an unknown need? (In some cases, the suspects don't know they can benefit from our services.)

Obviously, answering this question will eliminate more suspects. We're left with a group of *prospects* we have good reason to believe can use our product or service. Now it's time to narrow our pool of prospects into a list of *qualified prospects* by determining the answers to another set of questions:

- Can the prospect afford our product or service?

- Is he or she interested in acquiring our product or service, or can such an interest be developed?

- Is he or she aware of our products and services and how these products and services can benefit him or her?

A prospect who can't afford our solution obviously isn't a qualified prospect, because no matter how much he or she wants to purchase, he or she can't. Likewise, a prospect who does not (or will not) recognize the need for our service is also a short-term dead end. Although this narrowing process eliminates many prospects for immediate sales, these same prospects may be worth staying in contact with for a while, because their circumstances may change in our favor. Perhaps they'll acquire the means to purchase, the need will become apparent to them, or—in the case of a company—personnel changes may open up new opportunities to revisit the company's needs.

Now we're left with a group of qualified prospects who:

- Can afford our product or service;

- Have a genuine need or want for our product or service;

- Have some level of interest;

- Are aware of our particular company and what we offer; and

- Are willing to consider acquiring our product or service.

In most cases, by now we've made direct contact with the person or business and are beginning to develop a sales relationship. Of course, the final cut is from qualified prospect to customer. Those prospects who actually buy from us become our ultimate client group. We end up with a prospecting chain that looks like this:

The World of Entities
↓
Suspects
↓
Prospects
↓
Qualified Prospects
↓
Customer or Client

Most of the "referrals" salespeople receive come from group one— names and phone numbers, the world of entities. The referring parties come up with a name and phone number for someone they believe might have some interest in our products or services. This is usually someone they believe is safe. They tend to provide the name and number of someone who probably won't meet with the salesperson. Or they give the name of someone they don't know well, so they won't have to worry if things don't work out. Only 10% of the "world referrals" a salesperson receives actually result in a sale.

Not all referrals fit into the world category. On occasion, a salesperson is blessed by a referral to a suspect. In such cases, we've narrowed the field a bit and now have a prospect that seems to meet our basic criteria, at least on the surface. He or she is in the right geographic area, the right industry, and the right-sized company, and appears affluent enough to buy. The referring party has taken the time and has the confidence to give us a name and phone number that seems to fit our criteria. This time we have over a 15% chance of getting a sale from the referral.

Sporadically a client does refer us to someone he or she knows will benefit from our product or service. He or she has given us a referral to a true prospect. At this point we don't know if our product or service is the right choice for the prospect, whether or not he or she can afford to make the purchase, or if he or she is *aware* of the need for what we're selling. But at least we have a referral that does, in fact, need us. Our chances of closing a sale with this referral are almost 40%.

On rare but glorious occasions, our referring party will provide a name and phone number for a truly qualified prospect—someone who needs what we're selling, is aware of that need, and has the means to purchase. Our chances of generating a sale from this referral jump to well over 60%.

Referral Entities and Expected Closing Percentage

The World: Less than 10%
↓
Suspects: About 15%
↓
Prospects: About 40%
↓
Qualified Prospects: Over 60%

Let's return to the original question: What is a referral? Again, a referral is much more than a name and phone number. If we divided the so-called referrals most salespeople receive into categories we'd find that over 60% of referrals (names and phone numbers) fall into the "world" category; about 25% fall into the "suspect" category; and only about 15% are true prospects, or qualified prospects. Is it any wonder the average salesperson doesn't generate enough referrals to make a significant difference in his or her sales volume?

Yet most salespeople believe they're getting referral business by obtaining names and phone numbers. Unfortunately, this practice isn't much better than opening the phone book and picking names at random. Still, they *feel* they're getting referrals.

A real referral falls into either the prospect or qualified prospect category. The further down the chain the referral is, the more likely you are to make a sale. A typical salesperson's names and phone numbers translate into a 15 to 20% chance for a sale, whereas a salesperson who generates real, strong referrals will enjoy a referral closing chance of 45 to 55% or higher. That means, given the same number of referrals, a salesperson generating strong referrals will close three or four times more referred sales than the typical salesperson. And what happens if that salesperson generates two or three times more referrals than the typical salesperson? He or she will close 6 to 10 times more volume.

Our challenge, then, is to find a prospecting method that will generate a large number of referrals for the suspect and prospect categories. Better yet, we'd like to develop a method to consistently generate referrals that fall into the prospect and qualified prospect categories. In that case, we should dramatically increase our close ratio and sales volume—and possibly, decrease the amount of time we spend prospecting.

The obvious question is: Why do we need to create a system? Why not just ask customers and clients for referrals?

PERSONAL INVENTORY

Being honest with yourself, list every referral you remember receiving over the past year and categorize them as world, suspect, or prospect.

_____

_____

_____

_____

_____

_____

_____

Which of your customers gave you the most qualified referrals?

_____

_____

What, if anything, was different about your relationship with these customers?

_____

_____

Which of your clients can you reapproach for qualified referrals?

_____

_____

Simply Asking for Referrals Doesn't Work

By now I'm sure you're wondering, "How can I generate those important prospect referrals?" The traditional method for getting referrals is simple and straightforward—make the sale, do a good job, and ask for referrals. You'd think this method would be sufficient. What could be simpler than asking a satisfied customer for a referral to someone who might be able to use your product or service? The problem is, we've known for years this format just doesn't work. Using the "ask for 'em and get 'em" method of referral training—which is how most of us were taught—results in a large number of "world" referrals, a few "suspect" referrals, and hardly any "prospect" referrals.

Before we study the method of referral generation that *does* work, we need to explore why the traditional method of asking for referrals doesn't work. Understanding what's wrong with the traditional method will help us build a method that eliminates those issues.

One of the primary reasons for failure occurs with the basic referral question. Studies show most salespeople either don't ask for referrals, or they ask in such a manner that the customer doesn't understand the request. Despite what many salespeople tell their peers and sales managers, over 55% of customers surveyed claim their salesperson never asked for referrals. This doesn't necessarily mean the salesperson didn't ask—it could mean the customer wasn't asked in a manner he recognized as a request for a referral.

Customers surveyed often cited confusion regarding the referral requests they received from salespeople. They understood their salesperson's request as a secondary suggestion rather than a request. Examples of confusing requests were:

- "Tom, if you happen to know anyone else who can use my services, I hope you'll consider giving them my name and number."

- "Bill, here are a couple of my business cards. If you run across anyone looking for a home, just give them one."

- "If you think of anyone who could use me, I'd love to hear about them."

- "Let me know of anyone I could be of service to."

These are *not* referral requests. At most, they're suggestions; at worst they're nothing more than throwaway sentences your customers will forget almost immediately. Yet, these are the common methods sales-people use to generate referral business.

This actually reveals three issues we must deal with when constructing a referral generation system. First, we must ask for referrals. Rarely will a customer or client simply volunteer. Unless the client knows we need referrals and our business depends on referrals, he won't think about giving them—much less actually volunteer the information.

The most common reason salespeople don't ask for referrals is fear: fear of rejection by the client, or the fear of irritating a client from whom they're seeking additional business. Just as the fear of rejection can hinder your ability to prospect by cold-calling, the fear of being rejected by a customer inhibits the request for referrals. The fear that keeps a salesperson from asking for referrals puts him in the position of finding other ways to get new clients—and this may lead to additional cold-calling. All we're doing is trading one fear for another.

Is the fear of rejection justified? Not if you've done a good job for your customer, from initial contact to the final delivery of the product or service. Assuming the process has gone well, you have no reason to fear asking for referrals. When I ask salespeople why they don't ask for referrals, the usual responses are:

- "My customers don't know anyone who needs the products."

- "My clients are too busy to give referrals."

- "I don't want to mess up my chances of doing business with these clients in the future."

These are nothing but excuses for avoiding asking for referrals. How do you know a client isn't acquainted with someone who needs your product or service? Can you read your clients' minds? Making the assumption for your clients is dangerous business, both during and after the sale. You don't know who the client might know—and you won't find out unless you ask.

Your client is too busy to give referrals? Again, this is a common excuse for not asking. I've received referrals from CEOs of Fortune 50 companies, physicians, and others who are usually considered too busy to give referrals. Sometimes with this level of client, the referrals come in unusual ways. For example, a Fortune 50 CEO told me during our referral gathering meeting that he had to step into the other room for a few minutes, but if I'd go through his address book and pick out the names I was interested in, we could talk about them when he came back into his office. I was delighted. I happily spent 30 minutes working my way through the address book and came up with 11 great referrals. When he got back, we went over each name while I took notes. He then pointed out additional companies I should contact—firms I was unaware of at the time. Seven of those referrals turned into sales, yet my client spent only 20 minutes with me.

The last most common objection—not wanting to irritate a client and jeopardize future business—may be legitimate. If the sales process didn't go well for some reason, then asking for referrals might be risky. Much depends on what happened during the sale, as we will discuss later. But assuming everything went well, this objection is another excuse to avoid asking for referrals. Asking for referrals after performing well should not offend a customer. In fact, it's a compliment. Depending on who the customer is, you may offend him if you *don't* ask for referrals. If your client is in sales, he or she may expect you to request referrals and will wonder about your competence if you don't. Most top executives spent time in sales at some point in their careers. These executives will expect you to ask for referrals.

The second problem salespeople encounter in generating referrals is only asking once. Over 70% of clients surveyed indicated they either hadn't been asked for referrals, or the salesperson asked them only once or twice. Customers who were asked for referrals only once averaged giving 1.47 names and phone numbers, those who were asked twice averaged 2.03 names and phone numbers, and those who were asked three times produced an average of 3.28 names. These weren't referrals as we defined a referral earlier, but rather just "world" names and phone numbers. But at least those salespeople who asked for referrals twice received more names. Simply asking twice could double or triple your referral base. Using the referral generation method presented here can increase the average number of referrals to 4.84 per client—three times as many as asking once, and twice as many as asking twice. Plus, the referrals you get from this method are far more likely to purchase than the so-called referrals most salespeople receive. That's because our method specifically targets referrals from the "prospect" and "qualified prospect" categories.

So now we know what should be obvious: It's important to ask. But why don't customers give us good referrals? This is a more complicated question with several answers. In the end you'll need to analyze why each client gives poor referrals, but poor referrals usually result from one of the issues discussed in the following paragraphs.

The customer may feel you've put him or her on the spot. A typical referral request comes after the sale is made, during a post-sale discussion, and without any warning to the client. The discussion may go something like this:

SALESPERSON: "Well, Mr. Smith, I'm pleased, as I know you are, that everything went great."

CUSTOMER: "Yes, everything seems to have gone well."

SALESPERSON: "Do you know anyone else who might benefit from my products?"

CUSTOMER (*frowns and shrugs*): "Well, I don't really know."

SALESPERSON: "It would really help me out if you could refer me to a couple of other companies that might be able to use me."

CUSTOMER (*scratches his head*): "Well, you could call John Doe over at ABC Manufacturing. They're kinda small, but they might be able use your products"

SALESPERSON: "Great! Can you think of anyone else?"

CUSTOMER: "Try Glenda Buyer at Widgets Made to Order. She and I talked a couple of months ago and I think they just installed a system like yours, but maybe they haven't bought yet."

The customer has had about 15 seconds to think of referrals. He was put on the spot and only came up with two names and numbers—one for a company he believes may be too small, and the other for a company that probably installed a competitor's system. Two weak referrals. Of course you'll call and try to set up meetings, but these prospects don't look promising. Still, if you're a typical salesperson, you walk away feeling pretty good because you now have two referrals.

Trust is another major issue in gaining quality referrals. Is the relationship with your customer built on trust? Have you done everything possible during the sales process to instill trust? Even if the sale itself went well—everything was delivered on time with no installation problems and the system worked perfectly—did you do everything as promised? Did you call each time you said you'd call? Were you there on time, every time? Did you send everything? Did you make sure each promise was kept, down to the smallest detail? Many purchasing entities—individuals and companies—won't complain or even mention small instances when the salesperson didn't follow through. Maybe she called in the afternoon instead of in the morning; perhaps she was habitually a few minutes late for meetings or took cell phone calls during meetings. Although your customers probably won't mention these incidents, they may hesitate to send you to a friend or colleague they respect. After all, they don't want to embarrass themselves by recommending someone who won't live up to the next customer's expectations.

Expectation during the sales process is a prime area for customer disappointment. In the previous exchange, between the salesperson and Mr. Smith, the salesperson said he believed, "the process went great." Mr. Smith's comment was more reserved; he said the process "seemed to have gone well." A matter of semantics? Possibly. But it might also be a difference of opinion. Possibly Mr. Smith expected more than he received. Since the salesperson didn't inquire, we'll never know. If we don't meet a customer's expectations, we can't expect to get quality referrals. Mr. Smith's salesperson didn't take the time to find out exactly what Smith expected or why he made such a lukewarm comment.

From the client's point of view, a referral makes a threefold statement to the referred prospect: He's recommending your performance

41

as a salesperson, promoting your product or service, *and* making a statement that the referred prospect should trust his judgment. A quality referral depends more on your client's trust in you than on your actual performance. Your client is putting his credibility on the line. If you fail to live up to the referred prospect's expectations, your client's judgment will be questioned.

We must construct a system that:

- ensures the customer understands our need and desire for referrals;

- informs or asks for referrals more than once or twice;

- helps the customer by defining what a referral is;

- ensures we perform exactly as the customer expects; and

- generates a high level of trust in the client.

On the Internet site www.pwwrreferrals.com you'll find a discussion board where salespeople provide personal examples of how they've overcome a number of common—and unique—referral generation issues we've discussed in this chapter.

PERSONAL REFERRAL SELLING INVENTORY:

Are you uncomfortable asking for referrals?

_____

At what point in the sales process do you ask for referrals?

_____

What were the specific words you used with your last client when you requested referrals?

_____

_____

Do you do everything you commit to exactly as promised?

_____

How many times do you ask a client/customer for referrals?

_____

Rate your ability to quickly create a trust relationship with your clients on a scale of 1 to 10:

_____

If you rated yourself below an 8 on developing trust quickly, what steps can you take to increase your rating?

_____

_____

_____

_____

What do you believe is your biggest hindrance in building trust?

_____

_____

PWWR Referral Generation System Summary

The PWWR Referral Generation System is based on four simple rules: <u>P</u>lant lots of referral seeds during the course of the sale, <u>W</u>ater the seeds constantly, keep the referral garden <u>W</u>eeded, and then <u>R</u>eap your referrals after the sale.

I. **PLANT** referral seeds:

From the first contact with your prospect, let him or her know you're a professional salesperson and you work primarily from referrals.

During the course of the sale, consistently remind your customer that you work from referrals.

Let your customer know in direct terms that you'll be asking for referrals once the sale has been completed.

Remind your customer throughout the sales process that you will schedule a referral gathering meeting with him or her after the sale. Ask him or her to be thinking about who he or she will refer you to.

II. **WATER** the referral seeds:

Change your voice mail, email, and printed materials to include a statement about your referral-based business.

If you perform well, get your client's agreement to supply quality referrals after the sale.

Make sure your customer knows exactly what a quality referral for you is.

Keep every single promise you make—no matter how small.

Make trust building with your client your primary goal.

The best watering is done when you seek to meet your client's *exact* needs and objectives, not what you *think* his needs and objectives are.

III. **WEED** the referral seed garden:

Be proactive; make sure you understand your customer's exact needs, expectations, and priorities.

Address any problem or issue that arises during the course of the sale honestly and promptly.

Keep your customer fully informed every step of the way. Communicate with your customer on a regular basis—even if just to let him or her know all is well.

If at all possible, find creative ways to mitigate the effects of a problem or issue—or, better yet, turn problems and issues into opportunities to add value to the sale for your client.

IV. **REAP** the rewards of a large number of quality referrals:

Meet your client at a separate meeting just for discussing referrals.

Have a wish list of possible referrals to ask your client about during the referral acquisition meeting.

The weaker the level of trust between your customer and the person he or she refers, the stronger the referral method you need to employ.

CHAPTER

Establishing the Referral Relationship

Planting and Watering

Now that we understand why simply asking for referrals doesn't work and why most customers don't produce solid referrals, it's time to discover what *does* work. How can you create a relationship with a client that eliminates the issues discussed in Chapter 3?

The key is to construct a relationship in which both parties know exactly what to expect—and when to expect it. As we've seen, most problems in generating referrals are simply relationship and expectation issues. The client doesn't know what the salesperson wants, and the salesperson doesn't know what the client expects.

Developing a referral relationship works in virtually any sales situation where the salesperson and client have consistent, sustained contact. The easiest industries to establish these relationships in are those that traditionally use relationship selling as their base: Real estate agents, insurance and financial services, attorneys, mortgage bankers, business-to-business sales, consulting services, and the like. However, anyone who uses a sustained sales process or who has a continuous flow of repeat business can develop this relationship, such as furniture and automobile sales, office equipment and supplies, energy suppliers, and so on. Any salesperson that has more than just casual contact with customers will benefit from learning to develop a strong referral relationship.

Many salespeople feel it isn't a good practice to bring up the subject of referrals with a customer before completing the sale. Traditional thinking tells us that referrals are an *after sale* benefit and that we shouldn't broach the subject until a customer is completely satisfied. Our model turns that thinking around.

Before you can generate this relationship with customers, you need to create new ways of thinking and new expectations. As with much else in sales, the salesperson must first internalize the process and believe from within; otherwise, the customer won't accept it. This simply means you must convert yourself to a referral-based salesperson even before the actual referrals start rolling in. If you aren't convinced your sales business is truly referral based, how can you convince your clients? Selling is a confidence profession, and you can't project the confidence required to convince a customer if you can't convince yourself.

Even if your business generates few referrals at this point, and few of those are what we consider a real referral, you should approach your customers exactly as though your business is established on a predominantly referral basis. In other words, you act the part to become the part. You think like a referral-based salesperson to *become* a referral-based salesperson.

Enter each relationship with a new prospect expecting to receive a minimum of five solid referrals once the sale is complete. Know that your compensation is more than salary or commission. You are compensated for your time and effort by the money you earn from the sale *and* by quality referrals from your clients. You must believe you earn more than the dollars an individual sale generates. If you truly believe referrals are part of the compensation package you earn by meeting the client's needs, your confidence in asking for referrals—and asking for a large number of quality referrals—will shine through. Your air of confidence will communicate the importance you place on referrals.

This doesn't mean you should be cocky or demanding. With the proper attitude, you don't need to be arrogant. You simply convey assurance that the client is working with a professional who knows what he or she is doing, that you will meet and exceed his or her expectations, and that you fully expect him or her to help you find new potential clients who can profit from your professionalism and expertise. If you don't believe these things, why should your customer believe them? Again, you must act the part in order to become the part.

As basic as it sounds, the only way to become a professional who earns and deserves the reward of quality referrals is to *become* the professional who earns and deserves quality referrals. Becoming a professional requires you to dress the part, speak the part, reflect the part, and *be* the part.

Unfortunately for many salespeople, this isn't as easy as it sounds— even for men and women who've worked in sales for years. I've seen a software salesman show up to do a formal presentation at an executive meeting of a Fortune 200 company dressed in khakis and a polo shirt; a realtor dressed in sweatpants meeting a client who wants to purchase a million dollar home; and a pharmaceutical salesman arrive for a meeting with the CEO of a small clinic in jeans, a sport coat, and tennis shoes. It's hard for clients to take salespeople seriously, much less refer them to other professionals they know and respect, if the salesperson doesn't bother presenting himself or herself in a professional manner.

Likewise, I've known salespeople who curse like sailors, tell off-color jokes, denigrate their competition, show up late, and perform other tasteless, rude, or otherwise inappropriate behavior during the initial sales call. Such behavior is hardly appropriate after a relationship with the prospect has been established, much less during the initial sales call. These salespeople may get the sale, but should they be surprised if the client is reluctant to provide good referrals?

Be professional in all aspects of your sales life. You're asking a customer or client to ask one of his friends, family members, colleagues, or acquaintances to meet with you. He certainly won't do that if he suspects you might embarrass him—no matter how well you and your company perform, no matter how great your product or service is, and no matter how much he likes you personally. People will not put themselves in a position to be embarrassed. Most customers assume the people they refer you to will be less forgiving and more demanding than they were. Consequently, any behavior on your part that a customer had to overlook may prevent him from referring you to other people.

ESTABLISH THE EXPECTATION OF REFERRALS
FROM THE INITIAL CONVERSATION

From the first time you meet a prospective client, you need to set the expectation for referrals. You must let the client know how you work (or, if you haven't had the opportunity to establish many referrals, how you *believe* you work). Let's take three examples of an initial phone conversation with a prospective client.

1. For the first example, assume you're a salesperson whose business is primarily by referral, but supplemented with cold calls:

> YOU (*shortly after the beginning of the conversation*): "Mr. Smith, I called you today because, although I usually work only by referral, I ran across your name and believe that (my product or service) could greatly benefit your company."

You let the cold call prospect know up front that the call is an exception to your usual method of doing business—and that you typically work from referrals. As the relationship develops, you will revisit this theme.

2. In this example you've begun to generate a fair number of referrals, but your business is still primarily generated from other sources. In this case, you have the luxury of a walk-in customer:

> YOU (*after the initial greeting*): "I'm glad I can help you today. Normally I only deal with clients who've been referred to me, but I have some extra time right now and I'll be happy to work with you."

53

Again, you let the prospect know up front that this isn't how you normally do business. You've stepped out of your normal method of finding clients, but you're delighted to help him. This theme will become a constant throughout the sales process.

3. This time you're a salesperson who's just getting started with a referral-based business and have only generated a few referrals to date. This is a call to a lead your company purchased:

> You (*shortly after the introductions on the phone*): "Mrs. Smith, I called today because, even though I primarily work only by referral, I ran across your name and believe that (my product or service) could greatly benefit your company."

Obviously, this is the same wording as the first example. You're acting the part to become the part, and you will revisit the referral theme consistently throughout the sales process—and afterward.

In each instance, your approach is the same—letting the client know right away you work almost exclusively from referrals and this prospect is an exception. As long as you convey this information in a

---

Referral Generation Tip

Referral Seed Planting Is Never Completed. To be most effective in generating a large number of high-quality referrals, you need to plant referral "seeds" throughout the sales process. Mentioning referrals once or twice will not plant enough seeds to be effective.

friendly, matter-of-fact, conversational manner, the prospect won't be offended and you won't seem arrogant. However, if you do this incorrectly, you can alienate a prospect by making it sound as though you're doing him a favor by stooping so low as to work with him.

However you make the initial contact, your first conversation with the customer should emphasize that you're a referral-based salesperson and working with nonreferred clients is the exception for you, not the rule. This not only puts you in a special category in the client's mind, but also begins preparing him or her for the end result when you ask for referrals. Throughout the relationship you will continue emphasizing how you work, but the process begins when you first meet the client.

During your first conversation with the prospect, you should also explain why working by referral benefits him or her. First, let the client know your normal method of acquiring new clients is via referrals. Then explain that working through referrals helps him or her, because: (1) it allows you to better meet his or her needs and co-ordinate the details of his or her sale because you don't have to spend time looking for new customers; and (2) you have more time to keep up with changes and innovations within your industry, thus serving your customers better by offering the most up-to-date solutions. In other words, working by referral allows you to be a true professional as opposed to the average salesperson, who is primarily a marketer.

Take a few minutes and give serious thought to constructing a 30- to 40-word statement that explains your referral business status and how it benefits clients. Your spiel should be brief, to the point, and memorized so you can use it on the spur of the moment without having to think. Here's an example:

"I normally work with clients who've been referred to me, because not having to prospect for clients gives me more time for me to focus on my customers' needs." This 28-word sentence conveys the message that you're a referral-based professional because you care about your clients and want to spend time servicing them instead of prospecting for new customers. A cold-call statement might be:

"Mr. Smith, I normally work with clients who've been referred to me, because not having to prospect for a client gives me more time to focus on my customers' needs. But I came across your name, and I believe that (your product or service) can benefit your company by (doing whatever it does)."

Here's a walk-in example:

"Ms. Smith, I normally work with clients who've been referred to me, because not having to prospect for a client gives me more time to focus on my customers' needs. But I'm free right now, and I'd be happy to help you."

When calling a lead supplied by the company:

"Ms. CEO, I normally work with clients who've been referred to me, because not having to prospect for a client gives me more time to focus on my customers' needs. But it came to my attention that you and your company are considering (purchasing, using; your product or service). Since you're the type of company I really like working with, I wanted to call personally and offer my services."

Write your personal 30- to 40-word referral business description in the following space:

_____

_____

_____

_____

_____

Working from referrals is neither simply a time- and money-saving tool, nor only a way to increase your sales and income—working from referrals allows you to position yourself in a much different way. Once you adopt the referral-selling model, you promote yourself as a professional in your industry who, unlike the competition, spends little time prospecting and a great deal of time working for your clients. You position yourself as a top producer and leader in your industry. You position yourself as an authority in your area of specialty, and everything you do is designed to reinforce that position in your prospect's mind. Of course, in the beginning you will act as though this is true and communicate with your client as though it's true, even though you haven't yet attained that level. Act the part to become the part.

In every industry, corporate and individual customers appreciate working with a truly professional salesperson. And how do they recognize a true professional? The ultimate test is how you perform during the sales process, but people also form lasting opinions during your initial phone conversation and the first meeting. Those judgments are based on such things as how you come across on the phone—the power and confidence of your voice, how much you know about them, how you dress and carry yourself, your ability to listen and answer questions, and your *perceived* level of knowledge and experience.

57

Acting the part to become the part requires you to perfect each of these aspects:

- Practice your telephone voice until you come across in a powerful, confident manner.

- Research your suspect to make sure he or she can use your products.

- Dress to impress.

- Research areas you believe the suspect may question you about.

- Speak in a conversational, equal-to-equal tone of voice and the suspect will perceive you as an experienced professional.

Perception isn't everything: You must also perform. But at this point you're trying to establish a relationship with the prospect, so it's important to leave a positive, knowledgeable, and competent image of yourself in his or her mind. Weak links in any of these areas can undermine your ability to get referrals. If your claims of professionalism don't match your actions, dress, and communication skills, you may do more harm than good. The prospect may doubt your referral-based business claims, putting everything else you say in question.

Remember that selling is the sum of everything you do and say. Developing a referral-based business is one aspect of your sales business, and it must fit in with the rest of your business. If referral selling isn't believable within your selling framework, then you must either change the framework to make referral selling a viable part of your business, or eliminate referrals from your selling model. Likewise, if your presentation skills, product knowledge, or some other aspect of your business is weak, you must take the necessary steps to strengthen that area.

COORDINATING YOUR SELLING MODEL TO INCLUDE REFERRAL SELLING

Since referrals will become a primary part of your selling model, you need to coordinate all your communications to reflect this. Each communication should contain a subtle reminder to your suspects, prospects, and clients. This means changing your voice mail message, business cards, stationary, and even the signature on your emails. Each communication should mention the fact that you work on a referral basis. No need to beat your prospects and clients over the head with this concept, but a dignified reminder is appropriate.

Change the message on your office phone and cell phone to mention that you work by referrals. Here's an example: "Hello, this is _____ and today is (date); I'm either on the other line or meeting with a client. My clients and the referrals they send me are my most important assets and I take great pride in my professionalism and their confidence in me. I'll return your call today between ___ and ___ or ___ and ___. If you're a new referred client, please leave your name, your number, the best time to return your call, and the name of the person who referred you. If you're a client calling to refer someone, please leave his or her name and number and I'll contact him or her today at one of the aforementioned times. Thank you."

Your business cards, stationery, notepads, and email should also reflect your referral-based business. A tag line such as "Referrals allow me to serve you better," or "My business is built on referrals," or

Referral Generation Tip

Invest in Quality. What you print and what it's printed on becomes a messenger that communicates to your prospects even when you aren't around. Invest in high-quality printing and materials. No one wants to deal with a bargain basement salesperson.

"Thank you for trusting me with your referrals" should appear on every written communication you send a prospect or referral, including the signature on your emails. Don't use something cute like "I (heart) referrals," or "Referrals make my day." These only communicate that you're excited to get an occasional referral.

If you develop and print your own personal sales materials (brochures, fliers, and advertisements), these should also reflect your referral-based business model. The referral message should be clear and up front. With brochures, you can explain in detail why your business is unique to your industry and how that benefits clients. As with verbal references to your referral-based business, you don't need to beat your customers over the head to get your point across. But you do want to reinforce the fact that your business is referral based. Include a simple paragraph explaining why you work by referral and the type of prospect who is your ideal client. If you're in a general business (for example, a realtor who doesn't specialize in a particular neighborhood, price range, or type of property), then it's more difficult to describe your ideal client. But if you do have an ideal referral prospect, by all means identify it. The more information you provide, the better referrals you'll generate from prospects and clients.

> *Referral Generation Tip*
>
> **Refine Before You Print.** Once you've developed your new printed materials, get feedback from people whose opinions you respect. Make sure your materials communicate what you *really* want to say before you invest in printing.

DEVELOPING THE REFERRAL RELATIONSHIP

After your initial meeting with a prospect, you'll continue reminding him or her that you work on a referral basis. Part of your job at this point is to simply communicate this fact. Once the sales process moves forward and a sale is imminent, you'll begin talking in more direct terms about your expectation for referrals. If the prospect was referred to you, all the better, because he or she understands the process. If you acquired the prospect by a method other than referral, you'll need to accustom him or her to the idea of referrals. By the time you actually

> *Referral Generation Tip*
>
> **Concentrate on Your Best Referral Sources.** Spend the greatest amount of time and energy developing referrals from your best referral sources, even though they may not be your biggest dollar customers. Sometimes your smallest customers can provide the most high-quality referrals. Identify these customers and concentrate on generating a large number of referrals from them.

ask for names and phone numbers, your new client won't be surprised. In fact, he or she will be expecting it.

You should mention referrals at some point during each conversation with your prospect, but keep it subtle—a natural part of the conversation. For example mention in passing that you just came from meeting a newly referred prospect, you're about to go into a meeting with a new referral, or you've just been referred to someone your prospect might know. Don't invent things. If you lie and try to impress a prospect by name-dropping, you may ruin your chances with the prospect *and* the person you lied about. Prospects and clients are far more likely to talk about negative purchasing experiences than positive ones. You want your clients to give you referrals, not to bring up your name to others because you lied.

Throughout this chapter I've advised you, "Act the part to become the part." By that I mean you should present a specific image and a perception of how you do business. You mold your business into what you want by making it true in your own mind and your client's mind, even before the new concept becomes reality. That is, if you work your business as though you're a successful referral-based salesperson and if you do the things necessary to develop that business, the business will follow. I'm not suggesting you should lie to your customers or clients. Never tell a prospect or client you were referred to an individual or company you haven't actually been referred to. Don't pretend to have more experience than you actually have. Don't claim knowledge or ability you don't posses. Presenting yourself as a polished, successful professional and then following up with the service and performance to justify your presentation isn't lying. Boldly stating things that are not true *is* lying. Don't let yourself be caught in a lie. Not only is it bad for business—it's bad for your soul. Salespeople don't need to lie.

We need to present ourselves as competent professionals, equals to our prospects and clients, but there's no need to embellish our credentials or experience. Act and perform the part to become the part.

ONCE THE PROSPECT INDICATES A DESIRE TO PURCHASE

As you guide your prospect toward a positive decision to purchase your product or service, you'll also move into a direct discussion of referrals. Once the decision to purchase is made, the prospect should understand your expectation of referrals. This conversation should take place right away. At this point in the relationship, tell the client you appreciate his or her business and will do everything possible to ensure the purchase goes smoothly. Let him or her know you'll closely monitor each step of the process, keep him or her fully informed, and quickly deal with problems that arise. Remind him or her that working from referrals gives you more time to address *his or her* concerns. Then tell him or her that soon after the completion of the sale you'd like a short meeting to discuss other individuals or companies who could use your products. Ask your client to think about good referrals for you.

Referral Generation Tip

Never Stop Generating New Referrals. Selling is a high-energy activity. Success in sales requires you to continue developing a large number of prospects. Although generating prospects through referrals results in a much higher close ratio, never allow yourself to become complacent. You must focus on generating new referrals, no matter how full your pipeline may look today.

During each contact from then on, you'll remind the client of the upcoming referral meeting. At this point, just as at the beginning of the relationship, the reminders are just that—reminders. There's no need to overdo it; you're simply reminding him or her that after the sale you'll have a referral meeting and you hope he or she will keep this in mind.

Visit the *Creating a Million-Dollar-a-Year Sales Income* web site at www.pwwrreferrals.com for additional suggestions on developing communications for your voice mail and printed materials, plus ideas for integrating these into your normal selling methods. You'll also find a discussion board where other salespeople reveal approaches that work for them.

PERSONAL INVENTORY

With how many past clients do you have a relationship that will allow you to go back and ask for referrals?

_____

Do you believe you have the ability to create a referral business? That is, the ability to project the image, skills, and experience required to support your referral-based business claims?

_____

If not, in what areas do you need to improve before you can incorporate a referral-based business claim into your sales process?

_____

_____

_____

How, specifically, do you intend to make these improvements?

_____

_____

What is your timetable for making these improvements?

_____

Check off each of the following as you change them to reflect your new referral-based business model:

____ Office voice mail

____ Cell phone voice mail

____ Business cards

____ Email signature

____ Fliers

____ Brochures

____ Web site

____ Letterhead

____ Notepads

____ Thank-you cards

____ Invoices and/or proposal forms

CHAPTER **5**

Getting
Agreement
on Terms

Weeding the Referral Garden

During the conversation with your new client regarding referrals, you must reach an agreement on four key terms. Not getting agreement on any of these four areas may seriously jeopardize your ability to generate referrals from the client. Weeding the referral garden requires more than just addressing problems that arise during the course of the sale. You must also be proactive and prevent issues by fully understanding each customer's wants, needs, and expectations—and by making sure each client fully understands your expectations of referrals.

REFERRALS AS COMPENSATION

At this point in the referral conversation with your new client, you've already told him or her that referrals are part of the compensation you receive for your work. Now you need a verbal agreement from the client that he or she will help with referrals. Some salespeople even have each client sign a simple agreement acknowledging an obligation to provide referrals if the salesperson performs up to his or her standards. I don't recommend using such an agreement. Although it makes the referral obligation more real in the client's mind, it may also intimidate him or her. And since a large part of any good sales relationship is built on trust, asking the client to sign a promissory note implies you don't trust his or her verbal promise.

I recommend a simple statement such as, "Ms. Smith, as I mentioned, my business is built on referrals because they free me from the time-consuming chore of prospecting for new clients and allow me to spend more time taking care of business. I'll be devoting many hours to the details of your purchase, making sure no one drops the ball. I believe getting good quality referrals from my clients is part of my compensation for a job well done. Would you agree with that?"

Your simple statement should tell the client how you earn referrals (by providing exceptional service) and why referrals benefit him or her. Then ask for his or her agreement. Once he or she agrees with you, move on to the next subject.

What if Joe Smith doesn't agree or won't acknowledge your question? Probe to find what issue he has with your statement. As with the probing questions you ask during the sales process to uncover unspoken objections to your product, you need to find your client's unspoken objection to providing referrals. Many salespeople approach this subject with kid gloves, fearing they'll push too hard and unravel a sale that has just been consummated. Certainly you must use your best judgment. But if you've built a good relationship to this point, you

Referral Generation Tip

Know Your True Value. When you use the service and communication techniques in this book, your level of value-added service to your customer will be far beyond most of your competition. When you recognize the superior level of service you provide, you'll be less reluctant to ask for referrals. If your service is far above your industry standard, you have a right to ask for additional compensation in the form of referrals.

should have no fear of alienating your client by probing for his or her referral objections.

Most clients will readily agree with your statement and also agree with the obligation to provide referrals for a job well done. Those who hesitate may have an unspoken question about why they should compensate you with referrals when they just agreed to pay X amount of dollars to your company for the product. This objection simply means Joe Smith doesn't fully understand how he will benefit from providing referrals. You must revisit and clarify why referrals are in his best interest. Three questions about his purchasing experiences will help make your point:

- "In the past, have the salespeople you've worked with kept you fully informed each step of the way?"

- "Have you experienced coordination issues with your past purchases?"

- "In previous sales for (your type of product or service), have you had misunderstandings, missed deadlines, or specific issues (such as, software not performing correctly after installation)?"

After posing these questions, you're bound to uncover one or more areas where the client had problems. Once you've discovered problems from the past, explain that many of these issues probably occurred because the salesperson didn't have time to properly monitor and coordinate all aspects of the purchase. Why? Because he or she was busy prospecting for new clients. You, on the other hand, work from a referral base, spend little time prospecting, and therefore can devote more time to each purchase and ensure everything goes as planned. By giving up the prospecting time, you sacrifice potential income in order to service your clients. This sacrifice is rewarded through referrals. After hearing this simple explanation, most clients understand exactly how giving referrals benefits them.

WHAT IS A REFERRAL?

Once you and your client agree about his or her obligation to provide referrals upon completion of a quality job, you need to define the term *referral*. As we discussed in Chapter 3, a referral means different things to different people. It isn't fair to assume your client knows what a quality referral is for your business. Unless you define this term, you stand an excellent chance of getting just names and phone numbers. It may seem obvious to you what a good referral is, but don't assume the client can read your mind. Bad assumption!

Let's examine three real-world examples from salespeople who made assumptions about their client's knowledge:

Example 1: Alan sells accounting software designed for mid- to large-size manufacturing companies. At a trade show he met the CFO of a mid-size Midwestern manufacturer who showed interest in the product. During the next four months, he met twice with the CFO, and was then referred to the head of accounting who agreed with the CFO that the software was an excellent match for their needs. They signed a contract. Alan then began working with both the head of accounting and the IT department to have the software installed and customized for the company. During this time, Alan worked exclusively with these two departments and no longer dealt with the CFO. After the job was completed he sat down with the head of accounting and asked for referrals. She gave him three referrals to other manufacturing companies of about the same size.

Unfortunately for Alan, all three referrals were to the head of the accounting department in each company, not to the CFO. He was referred below the ultimate decision maker. Now he had to sell the head of accounting in each firm to get them to refer him *up* to the decision maker. He had a much more difficult sale than if he'd been referred directly to the decision maker. His mistake was twofold: first, he allowed himself to lose contact with the CFO—who could provide high-level referrals—and second, he didn't explain to the head of accounting what constituted a good referral. He made the assumption she knew, and she assumed he wanted a referral for her counterpart in another company. She thought the natural place for him to go was to the end user, not the decision maker.

Example 2: Darrell sells architectural millwork and cabinets to home and apartment builders. His product is modestly priced and appropriate for apartments and entry-level homes, his business is built on volume. The ideal customer for him is a volume builder seeking "nice" but relatively inexpensive product in large quantities. Although the majority of his sales are done on a bid basis, he does have clients who don't purchase based on bids, but on the quality and dependability of delivery and installation. One such client was a Texas builder who was building only his second apartment complex. Darrell worked directly with the two owners of the company. Upon completion of the project, he asked for referrals. He was referred to the two owners' previous employers. One owner had worked for an upscale homebuilder and the other for a company that built moderately expensive town houses. Neither would be in the market for Darrell's products. Again, if Darrell had explained what a good referral for him was, he might have received stronger prospects.

Example 3: Mika sells various health, life, and disability insurance plans to small employers. Her clients typically have between 10 and 49 employees, and her best prospects have between 20 and 40 employees. None of her clients have a human resources department, though most have someone designated as the HR person. Most of the time she sells directly to the business owner. Upon completing the enrollment of employees in the new health plan for a small trucking company, Mika sat down with the owner of the company and asked for referrals. The owner gave her the names of two business owners. One was the owner's sister, who owned a small company with only three full-time and seven part-time employees. The other referral was for a company with almost 80 employees. As with the other examples, the owner didn't understand what Mika needed. Like Darrell and Alan, Mika ended up with names and phone numbers that initially made her day—after all, she had a sale and referrals to two other companies—but she discovered the referrals didn't match her customer profile. This was a wasted opportunity that led to wasted time.

74

To make sure you stay on track with your referrals, prepare a short statement to quickly summarize your ideal prospect. The more specific you can be, the more likely you'll get the referrals you're looking for. If you sell to companies, your statement should describe not only the type of client you want, but also the client's specific title or area of decision authority within the company. Aim as high as possible in the corporation; it's always easier to get referred down the corporate ladder than bumped up the ladder.

Before moving on, take a few minutes and construct a brief, concise statement of your ideal referral. Since you'll be customizing this for each individual customer, state only the most important aspects of who you consider ideal:

_____

_____

_____

_____

Even if your ideal prospect is fairly general, you should still customize the information you give each client. For example, suppose you're a realtor who's happy to work with any buyer or seller within a reasonable distance of your office, irrespective of their income or the type of property involved. You've just sold a home to a married couple for $235,000. The ideal referral from them would be for someone in the $75,000 to $100,000 income bracket looking for a home in the $200,000–350,000 range. You want them to refer you to people just like themselves, because you assume they know other people who are approximately the same age, in the same income bracket, and live in more or less the same area of town. There's certainly nothing wrong with letting them know you work with a variety of real estate deals, but your specialty is people just like them.

75

No matter how you explain your ideal referral, you must give each client guidance on how he or she can help you. A referral isn't a referral unless you have a chance of making a sale. Don't allow yourself to be disappointed by receiving just names and phone numbers—and that's exactly what will happen unless you take the time to help each client understand what you mean by *referral.* Just as you need detailed information from your customer in order to meet his or her needs and objectives, your clients require detailed information from you in order to help you meet your goals and objectives. The less information you provide about what a referral is, the more general and higher up the prospect ladder their referrals will be. Help your clients help you by providing the information they need to identify potential customers for you.

NUMBER OF REFERRALS

How many referrals should you expect from your clients after a successful sale? The answer partly depends on your product or service. Five or six is a reasonable number of referrals for a financial advisor, realtor, loan officer, and other personal service professionals. Also expect five or six referrals if you sell a business-to-business product, such as health insurance or employee-leasing services. Salespeople in more specialized areas might find three or four referrals closer to the mark.

Decide for yourself how many referrals you can reasonably expect from each client, then communicate that expectation to your client and obtain his or her agreement. As with everything else in referral selling, it's important to make sure you and your client agree on this issue so there are no surprises on either side. The last thing you want—and certainly the last thing your client wants—are unpleasant surprises. Communication and performance are the keys to eliminating unwanted surprises.

Obtaining the client's agreement on the number of referrals you expect shouldn't be complicated or time consuming. Here's a sample statement:

"Great, Mr. Smith. I'm glad you understand that referrals give me more time to spend with my clients. I've found that most people can refer me to five new prospective clients, as I just defined them, without any trouble at all. Would you agree that five referrals is reasonable?"

Almost without exception, if you've mastered the calm, conversational, equal-footing approach, your client will quickly agree to provide five quality referrals. Don't try to negotiate a higher number of referrals than you actually expect to receive. If you want five quality referrals, agree on five. Trying to get agreement on eight with the hope of receiving five undermines your objective of building a relationship with your client that's built on trust and honest communication. Once you and your client agree on a reasonable number, assume that number will be provided at your referral gathering meeting after the sale is complete.

DEFINING A QUALITY JOB

Up to this point, you've spent four or five minutes discussing referrals with your client. You defined what quality referrals are to you, explained how important they are to your business, and agreed on the number of referrals your client will provide. Now it's time for one more step—the most crucial part of the conversation. Even if you decide not to adopt some parts of the referral generation model, this next conversation should be included in every salesperson's selling process.

You've agreed that the client is compensating you for a quality job by providing a large number of referrals. You must *earn* these referrals—they aren't given to you for nothing. If you and your company don't live up to your client's expectations, he or she has a right to withhold the agreed-upon referrals. But who decides whether or not you earned your referrals?

Before the sale proceeds any further, you and the client should establish what a quality job is and what's expected of each party. The traditional thinking about judging the quality of performance tells us to "do a good job" without discussing with the client what that means. Although a contract may stipulate the work to be done, when it will be done, and the end result, a contract doesn't define your client's underlying expectations. With or without a formal contract, each client has unspoken expectations. If these expectations are unreasonable, you need to educate the client on what he or she can reasonably expect.

Surprisingly, many salespeople neglect this area, believing they instinctively know what "exceeding the client's expectations" means. Ask most salespeople and their company executives about their sales performance goal and they parrot the current buzzwords: "exceed the client's expectations." Ask what that means and they'll tell you it means doing more than the customer expects. Ask what the customer expects and they'll say, "The customer expects timely delivery, no changes to the order, no major problems during the sale, and that the product or service does what is promised." Ask how they know this is

Referral Generation Tip

Put Your Client's Expectations and Priorities in an Email. Once you and your client have discussed his or her expectations for the sale, send an email restating those expectations and priorities, as you understand them. Ask the customer to either confirm or clarify them for you.

what their customers expect and they refer to experiences with previous customers. These salespeople and their companies may meet what they believe the customer's expectations should be, but they probably aren't meeting (or exceeding) what their client's expectations *actually are*. Don't be guilty of exceeding your own expectations but not meeting your customer's expectations because you don't really know what the customer wants and needs.

Few salespeople can state each client's specific expectations, because virtually no one directly asks the client what he or she expects. We tend to assume every customer is alike and they all have the same wants and needs. However, without knowing *exactly* what the client expects, how can you meet his or her expectations? Let me give three examples of salespeople who thought they performed well, yet still didn't satisfy their clients.

Example 1: Carlos sells pipe to oil companies. He sold a large order of pipe to a company in West Texas with a crew in New Mexico. The contract stated that Carlos' company would deliver the pipe in two shipments, approximately 1 week apart. Trucks from Carlos' company left the pipe yard at 7 in the morning on the day of the first delivery, beginning a 6-hour trip to the job site. Later that morning,

Carlos received a call from his client, who was furious. He wanted to know where the pipe was—he'd expected it on-site early that morning. The trucks arrived in the afternoon, but that wasn't good enough. Carlos was surprised and irritated at his client, because the man never said he expected an early morning delivery. Carlos believed he and his company were on time and doing exactly what they'd promised, whereas the client believed the pipe was late. Here we have an unhappy customer and an unhappy salesman, thanks to a lack of communication. Carlos failed to ask his client about specific expectations. Needless to say, Carlos made sure the second shipment reached the job site early on the appointed morning, but the damage was already done.

Example 2: Beth is a mortgage loan officer for a large bank and generates most of her business from homebuilder referrals. One of her builder clients referred a homebuyer (Mr. and Mrs. Dunn) to her for a mortgage on a spec home that was almost complete and would be closing in 2 weeks. While working with the Dunns, Beth learned they were missing one crucial piece of information—a recent bank statement. Since she didn't expect any problems with the statement, she didn't tell the builder about that minor problem. Instead, she told him the buyer was approved and closing would happen on schedule. The day before closing, she received the Dunns' bank statement. To her dismay, she saw a large, unaccounted for deposit during the past month. She needed documentation to explain this deposit before the bank could loan money for the house. She called the Dunns and learned that the deposit was a gift from their parents. They hadn't disclosed the gift, because they were afraid it would ruin the deal. Although this didn't disqualify the clients, they needed to obtain a gift letter and further documentation—a process that would take several days. Reluctantly, Beth called the builder and told him the closing would be delayed a day or two because the buyers tried to hide a gift. The builder was furious because he hadn't been kept informed. In his mind, the problem was *not* with the buyer for failing to disclose the gift, but with Beth for not telling him what was happening. Despite numerous smooth closings in the past with this builder, she now had to perform damage control because she failed to meet the client's expectations: She didn't keep him fully informed about a customer's loan.

Example 3: Lu Lin sells upscale home furnishings for a large furniture store in Florida. Her clients had just purchased a new home and bought several rooms of furniture to be delivered the day before they moved into the house. All the furniture was delivered on time and in good condition. Since the couple hadn't moved in, the builder's punch-out crew let the deliverymen into the home. They placed the furniture in the most logical rooms, removed the protective packaging, and carried off the packaging trash. That evening, Lu Lin received a call from an irritated buyer. The delivery crew had left a TV cabinet downstairs in the family room instead of upstairs in the master bedroom. The buyers would now have to hire someone to carry the piece upstairs, as it was too heavy for them to move themselves. A simple lack of communication jeopardized Lu Lin's chances for referrals from this customer.

I cannot emphasize it enough: You must know what your client considers a quality job, and then make sure you exceed those expectations. Most clients believe your performance should be above average in order to earn referrals—and sometimes their definition of "above average" is unreasonable. One software salesman installed a sophisticated management system for a client, a system that would then be customized to the company's specific needs. This process, including the beta testing, normally took several weeks. During the purchase negotiations, the contract was modified to cut the normal completion time by one-third—a tight schedule. Although the salesman carefully explained that the schedule would be difficult to meet and might be thrown off by any complications that arose, the customer had other expectations of what constituted a quality job. The salesman and his company met each deadline on time and the installation, beta testing, and final performance of the package met every requirement. The salesman was delighted things went well and assumed his client would be equally pleased. He was in for a surprise. The client acknowledged everything was on time and worked well, but he believed the salesman and his company simply met their stated goals and had not performed in an exceptional manner because they didn't complete the installation ahead of schedule. No matter that the installation was actually done in two-thirds the normal time. No matter that they had no significant hitches. No matter that the program performed up to expectation without bugs to work out. The client felt the installation was good, not great. Why? The salesperson had failed to identify this client's unrealistic expectations and deal with them up front. He and his company had, in fact, gone way above and beyond a normal installation, but the purchasing manager unrealistically believed things could have gone better.

Without a thorough understanding of what your client expects and how your client defines *quality job,* you run the risk of meeting and even exceeding your own expectations while failing to meet your client's ideals.

Gaining a complete understanding of your client's expectations and removing any unrealistic ones requires you to ask a number of detailed questions and take note of any area where misunderstandings may arise. It is incumbent upon you to make sure your client knows:

Referral Generation Tip

Forget What You Believe about Your Client's Expectations. Assume you know nothing about what a customer might expect during the course of a sale. Only by asking each client about his or her expectations will you know what he or she expects. Assuming you know will only get you in trouble.

- What's reasonable to expect and what is not

- What's normal within the context of your product or service sale

- What you will do out of the ordinary, if anything

The most common reason salespeople lose referrals is because they don't understand what the client believes constitutes a quality job. If you uncover unrealistic expectations, you must address them immediately and forcefully. Don't let your customer maintain expectations that cannot be met.

However, this doesn't mean expectations of unusually high performance are unrealistic. If your normal delivery schedule calls for delivery on a certain day, but any time during that day, you need to make sure your customer agrees to this. If your client insists upon delivery at a specific time during the day, you either have to eliminate that expectation (if your company cannot meet it), or agree to a specific time and meet that goal. Although it may be out of the ordinary for your company to commit to a specific time, if you do agree, don't expect your client to accept anything less. Some salespeople will agree to do almost anything to finalize a sale—even if they know they can't meet the request. These salespeople set themselves up to fail with their clients and they can't reasonably expect to get quality referrals. In fact, they probably won't ever deal with this client again because he or she won't give them return business.

Never commit to what you cannot deliver. If the customer's expectations exceed what you can actually do, you must replace this belief with a more realistic expectation. Once you bring the client's expectations into the open, you can usually arrange a compromise that will satisfy his or her needs.

As we'll discuss in Chapter 7, your goal is to meet and exceed your client's expectations at each point, during and after the sale. You can't do that unless you know exactly what the client expects.

The more complicated the sale, the more important it is for you and your client to prioritize objectives. Many sales transactions involve a number of operations, including delivery, product performance, training, and integrating with other systems or departments. Customers place different emphasis on these items, depending upon their needs. Work with your client to set priorities. Is performance more important than delivery? Is a timely delivery more important than budget? Is meeting criteria A more important than meeting criteria B? If one area must be sacrificed a little to meet the expectations in another area, what can be sacrificed and still allow you to meet the customer's primary needs? By helping your client prioritize objectives, you develop a framework from which you can develop contingency plans if any issues arise during the sale.

At www.pwwrreferrals.com you'll find examples of specific instances where salespeople encountered unrealistic client expectations and how they disarmed those expectations without offending the client.

PERSONAL INVENTORY

Are you comfortable telling your customers/clients that part of your compensation consists of referrals you expect to get from them?

_____

If not, why?

_____

_____

If you don't feel at ease explaining to your client that referrals are part of your compensation, what would help you become more comfortable describing this concept?

_____

_____

_____

Are you intimidated by asking for a specific number of referrals?

_____

If so, why?

_____

_____

How many referrals do you intend to ask for from each client?

_____

Is there anything that will keep you from asking?

_____

Do you take time to discuss expectations with each client and how he or she will determine if you've done a quality job?

_____

What are your weak spots in the following:

1. Your sales process _____

2. Communication _____

3. Follow up _____

4. Your company's performance _____

How can you pay particular attention to these details in order to ensure you meet your clients' expectations?

_____
_____
_____
_____

Have you had specific instances where you believed you and your company performed exceptionally yet your client felt otherwise?

_____

If so, can you pinpoint where the disagreements occurred?

_____

What could you have done differently to ensure the issue had not arisen?

_____
_____

CHAPTER 6

Negotiating
for
Referrals

Planting More Seeds

Virtually every sale includes some kind of negotiation. This may involve price, quantity, delivery, quality, split delivery, and a myriad of other items. Many of these items don't directly affect the salesperson's compensation, but they do affect his or her business— and possibly the timing of his or her commissions. If terms of the sale affect your income and ability to pursue other business, use this to negotiate with your client for additional referrals.

For example, a customer just placed an order he doesn't want delivered for 6 months—and you won't receive a commission until the delivery is complete. If your normal delivery time is 6 weeks but your client requests delivery in 6 months, you'll be forced to wait 4½ months for your commission. The client will probably agree to compensate you with a couple of extra referrals once you explain the cost of this sale to your personal income.

Take care that the client doesn't view your request as whining, complaining, or even extortion. If you negotiate for additional referrals in a clumsy manner, you could jeopardize your image and future business with the client.

Much of the material covered here requires practice as you polish your ability to communicate with customers. I recommend you perfect the basic referral relationship first, and then learn to negotiate for referrals. Here are the steps:

- Perfect your initial referral approach.

- Incorporate the referral concept into all your communications.

- Become completely comfortable with referral meetings where you gain agreement from the client that he or she will provide a certain number of referrals.

- Make sure your clients fully understand what a referral is for you.

- Make certain you fully understand each client's expectations—and he or she fully understands your capabilities.

At this point, you're ready to add referral negotiation to your sales toolbox. More than any other aspect of referral selling, this technique requires practice and confidence. You need to know each client well enough to anticipate his or her reaction. You don't want to look desperate or convey the impression that you're trying to take advantage of your client, and a poorly executed referral negotiation can easily come across that way.

Negotiating for Referrals

Once you feel competent enough to negotiate for referrals, you'll face three basic situations: (1) negotiating with a client for additional referrals due to an extraordinary circumstance with the sale, (2) negotiating price, and (3) negotiating with a client who originally refused to give referrals during your referral agreement meeting. These are discussed further in the following paragraphs:

1. The first type of negotiation is usually a straightforward discussion with your client. As in our example, you simply explain how the special request affects your business and suggest the extra burden will be lightened by a couple of quality referrals. If you read your client correctly, this should only take a minute or two.

2. Negotiating price offers the best opportunity to negotiate referrals. Price is always something of an issue for both parties. Many salespeople believe price is the primary negotiation term, though in reality it's usually second or third on the list. In many cases price is the least important aspect of negotiation, although it seems to draw the most attention.

Price negotiation offers a perfect opportunity to increase the number of referrals you can expect from a client. Since everyone expects give and take when talking price, you have the opportunity to bring in an unexpected negotiation term that offers the client a lower price, but costs him or her nothing in return—and gives him or her a chance to help others who may need your product or service.

Negotiating price requires you to withhold asking for additional referrals until you've approached your final price—the one you can't go below. For example, if you're selling an automobile, you probably started out somewhere close to the sticker price—or at least well above your company's bottom-line price. Most purchasers have a pretty good idea what they should pay for a particular car, so you both know where the negotiations will end. As you approach this final number, explain to the buyer that you work on commission and the price he or she wants to pay is so low that your commission will be close to nothing. In many cases this is true. It isn't unusual for a new car salesperson to end the transaction with a commission of $250 or less—sometimes much less.

Remind the customer that although you're about to give him or her a deal that strips away most of your commission, you *do* receive a bonus for sales volume (again, this is probably true, as most dealers give bonuses for selling over a certain number of units in a month). Tell the customer you'll be happy to approach your sales manager for approval of a sale below the accepted norm, *if* she'll give you an additional number of quality referrals.

Your offer is fair to the customer, who will save money on her car purchase for the price of referring you to a few more friends or acquaintances who may save as much as she did. It's also fair to you, because you may add a sale or two to your monthly quota, helping you reach the bonus level. It's fair to your company as well, giving them the potential for more sales. This is a win/win/win situation—all for the cost of a few names from the buyer.

As with other aspects of referral selling, negotiating for referrals isn't a lengthy process. It only takes a few minutes to explain how you work and ask the customer to offset your commission by providing more referrals. If you've already built a strong, trusting relationship with the customer, he or she will readily agree to give you extra referrals. You'll seldom receive a negative answer.

3. Negotiating with clients who originally declined to provide referrals is much more delicate. These are the clients who are most likely to feel uncomfortable with your request or view your referral negotiations as desperation. When a client has already said "no" to referrals, be careful about broaching the subject again. If you're in doubt about how a client will react to being reapproached, even during a negotiated referral, it's better to pass on the opportunity.

In order to reapproach a client about referrals, either during negotiations or after you complete the job, you need to know why he or she declined to give referrals during your referral agreement meeting. Possibly you failed to build a trusting relationship with the client, or perhaps he or she was afraid he or she would be committed to giving referrals even if you didn't earn them. Maybe the client truly believes that he or she doesn't know anyone who'd benefit from your product. Some clients might be uncomfortable about the product or service you sell. Prearranged funeral services, certain types of insurance, and other personal service items are more intimate than automobiles and pipe. The client may not want others to know that he or she purchased these things. This is an especially difficult objection to overcome.

If you investigate the reason for a client's initial refusal and believe you've brought the relationship to a point where you can reapproach him or her without creating hard feelings or causing him or her to question your motives, then move forward with referral negotiations. Approach this client the same way you'd approach anyone who agreed to referrals during the referral agreement meeting, but you're asking for additional referrals during the negotiation process. This requires nothing more than a simple statement of fact, a request for referrals, and waiting for the client to agree.

If the client again refuses to give referrals, don't ask again until well after the sale. You can certainly probe to find out why he or she said no, but trying to push the subject will be self-defeating. At some point—probably after a second sale to this client or well after the initial sale when your relationship with the client has been well established—you can approach him or her again for referrals.

At www.pwwrreferrals.com you'll find real-world examples of successful—and unsuccessful—negotiations. I analyze the failed negotiations, explaining what went wrong and how to prevent these mistakes. These examples will sharpen your skills and help you think through issues that arise with your own negotiations.

Earning
the
Referrals

Deep Watering

The old cliché of "under-promise and over-deliver" is particularly true for referral selling. As mentioned previously, exceeding the client's expectations is the number one commandment in sales, yet few salespeople actually do this because they don't know what their clients really expect. If you help each client define the meaning of *quality job,* then you know the minimum you must do to earn their referrals. Your real job is to exceed those expectations.

KNOW YOUR WEAKNESSES

Every salesperson and company has areas that may become issues during (or after) a sale—and in many cases these weaknesses are exactly where the customer has high expectations. Depending on your product or service, the weakness might be delivery, customer service after the sale, product dependability, product adaptability, ease of use, or any of a hundred other details. Make sure you're aware of your company's vulnerable areas and pay extra attention to them throughout the sale, and after it has been completed. If you tend to slip when it comes to keeping clients fully informed, make sure you communicate on a regular basis. Set up an automated tickler system that reminds you to call your clients. If your area of weakness is procrastination in delivering bad news, make a commitment to communicate that information within X number of hours from the time you receive the information. If your company often finds itself behind schedule because of overbooked production, negotiate a longer lead time to guarantee you can live up to your promises. Know your areas of strength and sell those, but also know your weaknesses. Head off problems by giving special attention to shaky areas and negotiating around them if possible.

It's inexcusable for a salesperson to create issues because he or she failed to address personal or corporate weaknesses he or she was aware of before the sale. Many salespeople will commit to things they know they can't do in order to make a sale. Then they pray things will miraculously fall into place. Other salesmen know their lack of com-

Referral Generation Tip

Communication Will Defuse Most Sales Issues. Simply keeping your customer fully informed in a timely manner can defuse most issues that arise during the course of a sale. Keep your customer informed and keep yourself out of trouble.

munication or coordination caused issues in the past, yet they don't take steps to correct these problems.

Selling is a proactive profession. Rather than setting yourself up to fail, address your weakness and help find solutions to problems within the company that affect your customers. If you foresee a problem, such as a delivery date that can't be met, it's better to immediately call your client and work out a solution, rather than wait until the last minute to break the bad news. Most clients understand about problems if you give them enough forewarning to make other arrangements. Don't put your customers in an untenable position by keeping them in the dark.

CONCENTRATE ON YOUR CLIENT'S PRIMARY OBJECTIVES

During the expectation discussion, your client will tell you what areas are most important to him or her. If you pay attention you'll also hear the client's secondary concerns. It's common to hear such statements as "My biggest concern is having the project come in on time. I can sacrifice a little performance from your software if I have to, but the project must be finished by X date"; or "Our most crucial need right now is to fund the college account for Suzi. The retirement plans we spoke of are important, but if you don't think we can afford to fund both accounts at this point, then concentrate on the college fund." These clients have just told you what is most important to them, and what comes second. Unfortunately, many salespeople don't hear these statements. In their desire to wow the client, they only hear "the project must come in on time" and "I'm concerned about Suzi's education and our retirement."

99

In addition to recognizing the spoken primary and secondary priorities of customers, train yourself to recognize a customer's implied priorities. Not all priorities will be voiced, but often they can be inferred from what the client doesn't talk about. It isn't just what a client says—what he or she doesn't say is equally important.

Although selling should be more about listening than *talking,* the art of listening escapes many salespeople. Most people view salesmen as good 'ol boy, hail-fellow, well-met types. In the real world, these salespeople gain many acquaintances, but few sales. Some of the most successful salespeople I know are quiet men and women who don't say much during a conversation, but the contributions they do make are well thought out and to the point. Force yourself to listen more than you talk. If you're talking more than 40% of the time, you're talking too much.

Returning to our previous two sales scenarios, the ideal sale would meet all the customers' criteria. However, the software and investment clients both gave specific instructions on what could be sacrificed from their sales. By the time these conversations took place, the salesperson involved should have formed a fair idea of whether both goals could be met. The moment he or she knew something had to be sacrificed, it was time to have a serious discussion with his or her client. As the work progressed, the salesperson should remember each client's primary and secondary objectives and concentrate on the primary objective.

It doesn't make sense for a salesperson to spend a lot of time meeting the secondary goal if that means sacrificing the client's primary objective. Meeting both objectives is a plus, but focus first on your client's highest priority; it's the first step toward meeting and exceeding his or her expectations.

EXCEEDING EXPECTATIONS

Of course exceeding a client's primary and secondary objectives isn't the only aspect of the sale. The expectation discussion with your client gives you an opportunity to discover his or her hot points. Be alert for such comments as:

- "If you can't do X, I need to know as soon as possible."

- "I don't want to lock in my rate right now, because I think rates are going to go down. If you believe rates will rise, please let me know immediately."

- "If your engineers think they might have problems integrating this software with our system, please let me know so I can set up a meeting with our engineering department."

I'm sure you already hear statements like these from your clients—and I hope you pay attention to them. More salespeople get into trouble with clients because of poor communication than all other areas combined. Performance is important, but communication is critical. Most performance issues can be dealt with and disarmed by keeping your client fully informed about what's happening with his or her order. It's that simple and that difficult.

Will your delivery date be missed? Inform the client at the earliest possible moment. Engineering issues? Inform the client at the earliest possible moment. Integration problems with the existing system? Contact the client at the earliest possible moment. Interest rates look like they're about to go up? Call the client. Home buyers are having issues qualifying for the loan? Call the client as soon as possible. The factory delivered a chair with the wrong fabric? Inform the client as soon as possible.

Procrastination kills referrals. Salespeople hate delivering bad news, and many subscribe to the idea that "no news is better than bad news." Yet your client can't work around a problem if he or she doesn't even know there *is* a problem. Hoping things will somehow work out only worsens the issue, until eventually the salesperson has to call. By then it's usually too late to find a workable solution. Whether or not you decide to use these methods for obtaining referrals, you should develop a system to keep your customers fully informed.

Exceeding your customer's expectations often means nothing more than communicating honestly and in a timely manner. Most clients are not unreasonable. People understand that unexpected things may happen during the course of a sale. But they won't understand lack of communication. Good communication can make up for a multitude of other sins during the course of a sale. Exceeding a customer's expectations often requires just picking up the phone, or sending a timely email.

Client communication is a discipline issue each salesperson must address. Developing the self-discipline to deliver bad news is difficult, because we naturally assume negative news will impact our relationship with the client. However, negative news doesn't have to be delivered by itself. If you work out one or more potential solutions before calling the client, you may be able to mitigate the impact of your news and, on some occasions, turn the negative into a positive. Too often a sale is damaged not by the problem itself, but by how the salesperson delivers (or doesn't deliver) the news.

If you and your client had prioritized his or her objectives, you'll have a basis to explore solutions to issues that arise during the sale. The solution may take considerable effort and creativity on your part, but understanding your client's primary objective will greatly improve your chances of developing an alternative plan.

One of my seminar attendees sells wholesale products to gift and specialty stores. A few years ago at a pre-Christmas market, her company was the exclusive U.S. distributor for three new gift lines. Two of these lines were expected to be among the year's best-selling new products for gift stores. Both product lines were limited to only a few gift shops in each market area, and one of the lines had already closed to new stores. One of her clients came in and immediately signed up to sell the remaining "hot" gifts—a line of ceramics scheduled to ship to the United States from China just in time for the Christmas selling season. To everyone's dismay, the ship carrying the initial shipment sank on the way to the United States. There would be no product for the first half of the selling season.

Knowing how important this gift line was to her customer, the account representative worked with her company and found a solution to the problem before she called the client. She knew the client's primary objective was to have a hot seller with limited competition. The account rep managed to get her customer approved to sell the gift line that had been closed. The bad news she delivered to her customer actually turned to her client's advantage. Her client would immediately receive a shipment of the newly approved product and still receive a shipment of the original line during the Christmas selling season. Her customer ended up with two of the year's strongest sellers instead of one, with one arriving at the beginning of the selling season and the other in mid-season. By knowing and concentrating on the client's primary objective rather than on a particular product, the account rep not only salvaged the relationship with her client, she helped her client generate one of the store's most successful Christmas seasons.

SERVICE PARTNERSHIPS

Many salespeople, such as realtors, mortgage loan officers, investment brokers, attorneys, accountants, and financial planners, must integrate their services with other vendors. The vendors you're associated with, whether by choice or chance, have a direct bearing on your ability to deliver services to your client as promised. Salespeople often choose their service partners based on friendship, cost to the client, or some factor other than the vendor's quality of service. Customers usually view service partners as extensions of your service—even if you had no say in choosing that service provider. Since many transactions requiring multiple service providers are fairly complicated, the explanation of where and why a breakdown occurred is immaterial to a customer (and often confusing since it isn't unusual for the customer to receive conflicting stories as to who was at fault and why). It's in your best interest to take the selection of service partners seriously and base your choice on the level of service they provide and their willingness to integrate their systems with yours.

When you're expected to work with a service provider you know cannot or will not do the job properly, it may be in your best interests not to deal with them—even if that means giving up a piece of business. This is a hard rule to maintain, but the damage done to your reputation by working with someone you know is incompetent may outweigh the value of the immediate income. Maintaining your integrity and discipline in the face of losing a paycheck may be difficult—especially for struggling salespeople—but it will pay dividends in the future.

As a mortgage originator and manager in Houston, I made decisions each day about who I'd work with. Some providers couldn't seem to handle even the simplest transaction. I found others in whom I had complete confidence, and I used them at every opportunity.

For example, I found an excellent title company and worked with them as often as possible. In the mortgage industry a competent title office is one of our most important allies. In Texas, the title office is responsible for generating the title commitment, closing the transaction, and disbursing the monies. From the mortgage originator's point of view, the most critical items associated with using a title office include:

- How long it takes the office to generate the commitment

- How they treat the realtor, mortgage originator, and client

- How quickly and well they address title issues

- How efficiently they close the transaction

Over the years I'd worked with many title offices and escrow officers. Most were efficient, some more so than others. But I eventually found an office owned by Richard Crow, a real estate attorney who owns a Stewart Title Fee Office in Houston. Richard is efficient, goes out of his way to take care of clients, offers free services that other companies charge clients for, and treats everyone as though they're his only customers. Because Richard's office did such a great job, I knew that my clients and my loan officer's clients would receive a level of service that complimented the service I provided and that reflected well on me. Over time Richard also became a friend. His office became a virtual extension of my office. And Richard still treats every mortgage loan officer and realtor the same; everyone who uses Richard feels as though they're his only client.

Not only can service providers help make or break your business, they should also send referrals your way, just as you refer to them. Once you establish a relationship with a provider you trust, begin the referral conversation and develop them into a referral source—just as you would with any other client.

PERSONAL INVENTORY

Before proceeding to the next chapter, take a few minutes to examine yourself and your company. Make a list of strengths and weaknesses:

Your strengths:

_____

_____

_____

_____

_____

Your weaknesses:

_____

_____

_____

_____

Your company's strengths:

_____

_____

_____

_____

Your company's weaknesses:

_____

_____

_____

_____

How can you overcome your personal weaknesses?

_____

_____

_____

How can you overcome your company's weaknesses?

_____

_____

_____

How effective are you in determining your customer's primary and secondary objectives?

_____

_____

If you've had difficulty distinguishing between primary and secondary objectives, what steps must you take to ensure you fully understand each client's objectives?

_____
_____
_____
_____
_____
_____

Do you have a system in place that ensures you keep your customers fully informed of the status of their purchase, including negative news?

_____

If not, what system can you put in place that will ensure complete and timely communication?

_____
_____
_____
_____
_____

CHAPTER

The Referral Acquisition Meeting

Reaping the Referrals

Your reward for the hard work of selling a customer, developing a strong referral-generating relationship, and making sure the customer's expectations are exceeded comes when you meet with the customer and receive high-quality referrals.

If you or the customer approach this acquisition meeting with little preparation and planning, the result will be disappointing. Having spent a great deal of time building a relationship with the client, you must give yourself the best opportunity to take advantage of the referrals you receive. Planning and executing a smooth referral acquisition meeting can increase your closing percentage with the referred prospects by as much as 100, 200, or even 300%.

PLANNING FOR THE REFERRAL ACQUISITION MEETING

Set an appointment with your client specifically for a referral meeting. Salespeople often try to integrate the referral acquisition meeting into a general post-sale meeting. This format doesn't do justice to the importance of your referrals. If you try covering several topics at the same time, you risk not having enough time for the referral portion of the get-together because other topics may take more time than you expected—and the client may try dodging the subject. Setting a specific referral acquisition meeting makes the agenda clear to your client, emphasizes the importance you place on referrals, and eliminates diversionary topics and issues.

Occasionally you'll show up for the referral meeting and find your client has other issues to be taken care of—a question about your product or service, an issue within his or her company that needs attention, or any number of other distractions. In such cases, reschedule the referral discussion for a time when you can have your client's undivided attention. If your client's issue has to do with your product or service, simply change the day's topic to address his or her needs and concerns, then suggest a reschedule time for the referral get-together. If his or her concerns don't have to do with you, acknowledge the issue and suggest the meeting be rescheduled. You want 20 to 30 minutes of your client's total attention.

When you arrange the meeting, let your client know exactly what to expect. Inform him or her that:

- the meeting will be short (20 to 30 minutes)

- he or she should be prepared with names, addresses, and phone numbers of the referrals

- you'll be asking a few questions about each referral

- you may have a few potential referrals to ask about

Before the meeting, develop a list of potential prospects your client might know. For instance, if your client is the VP of sales and marketing for a telecommunications company, you might come prepared with the names of his or her counterpart in several other companies that interest you. You might develop a list of decision makers who work for your client's company as vendors or with firms your client's company supplies. If the client doesn't bring up these names during the meeting, ask if he or she knows them and can refer you to someone. Don't assume your client doesn't know these people—they might have simply slipped his or her mind. And don't assume your client will be offended if you ask about these names.

Use all of your resources to prepare for an acquisition meeting. For instance, while selling a package of sales training seminars, I discovered during a conversation with the CEO that he'd been division president of another large company. I already had an interest in this company and hoped the CEO would give me a referral. When he didn't mention the name during our referral acquisition meeting, I asked if he knew the current division president and would be comfortable contacting him.

He said, "I don't know the division president, but I know his boss, the president of the company—and I'll be glad to refer you to him."

From that referral I had the opportunity to sell my services to three of the company's divisions, not just one. Another example of taking advantage of resources for an acquisition meeting came from one

113

of my seminar attendees, Heather. Her client, Mary Smith, was vice president of operations for a large call center and had just purchased several expensive copier/printer/scanners for a major expansion. During Heather's conversations with another prospect, she discovered Ms. Smith had worked for a large firm as second in command of their local call center and had left the company on good terms. In fact Ms. Smith's former company was trying to hire her back. Heather used this information during her referral acquisition meeting; she asked Ms. Smith for a referral to the other company. Ms. Smith agreed, and the referral produced a good contact with one of the area's largest firms. Heather obviously knows how to ask the right questions at the right time.

What if you need referrals for people instead of companies? Joan, one of my seminar attendees, sells cosmetics. She found out during a conversation that one of her customers belonged to a women's business organization. Before the referral meeting with that customer, Joan tracked down a copy of the organization's membership and came prepared with a list of 40 names. The customer arrived with 6 referrals; by the time the meeting ended, Joan had referrals to 27 potential customers. Twenty-five of those names came from the membership list.

Using industry-specific magazines and newsletters for your client's industry can help you generate a list of companies your client may be able to refer you to. Go to www.pwwrreferrals.com and you'll find an extensive list of publications and links to each magazine's web site or a site where they can be ordered.

GATHERING REFERRALS

During the referral acquisition meeting, your primary job is to gather specific information about the referred prospects. The more you know about each prospect and his or her needs, the better. Take each referral your client gives you and spend a few minutes asking questions such as:

- How long have you known the prospect?

- How well?

- In what capacity?

- If the referral is to a specific person within a company, ask about that person's authority to make the appropriate decision, how long he or she has been with the company, and his or her work history.

- If your client isn't sure about someone's decision-making authority, ask if he or she can refer you to that person's boss.

- What does the client know about the company—specifically its reputation, profitability, current use of your product or service, recent growth (or downsizing), and any other factor that might be of interest to the sale of your product or service?

Once you've asked specific questions, finish the discussion of each prospect by asking your client why he or she is referring you to this person. Hidden in his or her answer, you'll often find your primary sales approach.

Referral Generation Tip

Thank Your Client for the Referrals. After your refer-ral gathering meeting, send you client a thank you note and promise to keep him or her fully informed on each referral he or she gave. Then make sure you keep your promise.

If the referred prospect is an individual rather than someone within a company, your questions will be much the same. As with a corporate prospect, finish the meeting with an open-ended question about why the client chose to refer this particular prospect. You want to learn everything you can about each prospect or company. You're looking for information that will help you connect with an individual, show you how to *sell* the prospect, and help qualify him or her. Of course, you won't gather every piece of information you'd like, but spending 5 or 6 minutes on each prospect should give you a good idea of who the prospect is, how you might be able to help him or her, and how qualified (or unqualified) he or she is to make a purchase.

When your client finishes telling you about his or her referred prospects, ask about the prospects on your "wish list"—potential prospects you prepared during your research before the meeting.

Above all else, you must get an idea of how strong the relation-ship is between your customer and the person he or she is referring. The stronger the relationship, the less selling you'll have to do—and the better chance you have of gaining an appointment. As we will see shortly, the strength of the relationship has a major impact on how you'll approach the prospect.

Referral Generation Tip

Keep Your Referral Source Fully Informed. Clients want to know how their referral is going. Keep your client fully informed about what's happening with each referral he or she gave you. And make sure the client is aware of any problems before he or she has a chance to hear about it from the referred party. Clients don't like unpleasant surprises from the people they referred to you.

WHAT IF YOUR CLIENT DOESN'T HAVE REFERRALS?

You must be prepared for the occasional client who, despite your best efforts to prepare him or her in advance—and despite his or her agreement to help you—shows up for the meeting without any referrals. Perhaps he or she will offer the lame excuse that he or she doesn't know anyone who's interested.

This situation is frustrating, but don't let it discourage you, and don't allow yourself to express frustration or anger. Take a deep breath. Stay calm. Begin the meeting by going over the list of potential prospects you prepared during your research for this session. When you finish the list, inquire if the client would mind going through his or her Rolodex with you. Many people have plaques or membership books in their office from civic and professional organizations. Ask the client if he or she knows anyone in those organizations who'd be interested in your product. If the client works in a large company, ask about other departments or subsidiaries that might need your product or service.

Working your way through your "wish list," your client's Rolodex, the organizations he or she belongs to, and other areas of the company should generate several good referrals. If, after all this, your client still can't provide several quality referrals, schedule another appointment with him or her. Remind him or her why referrals are important to you and ask how you can help him or her prepare for the next meeting.

Probe your client to find out what's preventing him or her from giving you the referrals you earned. If your client has an unresolved issue with your product or service, he or she may not want to give you referrals.

REFERRAL CONTACT FORMATS

Acquiring the names, numbers, addresses, and specific information about referred prospects and their companies is the first step in the referral acquisition meeting. The second step is determining how you should contact these people. Each format has certain advantages and disadvantages.

Name, Address, and Phone Number

Most clients will give you this information. Although quick and easy, this is the least effective referral format because it makes you do all the groundwork in establishing a new relationship. Your goal is to establish a relationship with the newly referred prospect based on the trust and commitment of your client. Unless your client has a close, positive relationship with the prospect, calling out of the blue and using your client's name, or a letter mentioning your client's name with a follow-up phone call, is only slightly better than a cold call. If your client has a casual relationship with the prospect, this format may do nothing more than allow you to speak to the referred party. It probably won't make the prospect accept you as someone he or she should meet. In most cases, you need to make up for a weak relationship between your customer and the referred person by using a stronger referral format.

Email from Client to Prospect

In today's Internet-savvy world, your client may wish to contact the prospect via email to introduce you and your company. I strongly recommend you avoid this format. Emails are usually seen as casual communications, often briefly scanned or deleted without being read—even messages from friends and acquaintances. If your client insists on using email, ask if you can write the text for him or her. Provide a simple Word document with appropriate spaces left blank for the prospect's name, and then email the form letter to your client. He or she can fill in the blanks to personalize the letter with the prospect's name. As with all email communication, the subject line is critical. Let your client choose from a couple of subject line headings that have impact and will cause the prospect to read the email. If left to their own devices, most clients will send out referral emails with subject lines such as, "Referral," or, "This May Be of Interest." These are weak and will probably be deleted. Encourage your client to use strong subject lines, such as, "John, would you believe I found a way to increase sales by 23% this quarter?" or, "Gloria, here's my new car . . . You'll die when you see how much I saved!" Of course, almost anyone would delete these emails if they were spam, but coming from someone the prospect knows and trusts—well, that's a different matter. They will spark interest and readership the spammers only wish they could generate.

Personal Letter from Client to Prospect, Written by the Client

A personal letter written by your client on his or her letterhead is an effective way to contact your referred prospect. Assuming the prospect knows your client well, the letter will get past gatekeepers and will be read, or at least scanned, by the prospect. The personal letter is effective because it's rare; seldom, if ever, do people receive a letter of recommendation and introduction from someone they know and trust. Encourage your client to include details about his or her impression of you and your company's integrity and ability, a testimony about the product/service, and why the client believes the prospect should meet you. The more specific and detailed the letter, the more trust the client can generate on your behalf. Ask your client not to date the letters and to let you mail them yourself. When you know exactly when a letter is mailed, you can plan a follow-up phone call within several days. Don't mail a letter unless you can follow up immediately (within 3 to 4 days after it's mailed). Also ask your client for permission to make copies of the letters to use as general testimonials. Keep them in a binder you can show future prospects. This is especially effective if the client, his or her company, the prospect, or the prospect's company is a well-recognized name.

Personal Letter from Client to Prospect, Written by You

Far better—and probably more realistic than having your client write a letter of introduction—is for you to write the letter on his or her stationary and ask him or her to sign it. You're in a better position than your client to write this letter because you've already gathered a great deal of information about the prospect and you can describe how your product will benefit him or her. As with the client-written letter, be sure you specify what you did for the client, what results the client experienced, and what you can do for the prospect. Don't overstate or embellish your accomplishments—write as you believe your client would communicate. If you put words into your client's mouth, you risk not only losing the referral, but also his or her trust.

Personal Phone Call of Introduction by Client to Prospect

A phone call is even more powerful than a letter of introduction from your client. A phone call has the emotional impact of the letter—a highly unusual event—plus the added benefit of letting the prospect ask specific questions of both you and your client. Introductory phone calls tend to be relatively short and very cordial. The call guarantees you'll get to talk with your prospect (assuming he or she is available) and allows you to be introduced in a no-pressure atmosphere. Your chances of securing an initial meeting are high, because most people find it hard to say no to an appointment when the referring client is the one asking. Unfortunately, the prospect must be available for the call when both you and your client are together, making this a hit-or-miss proposition. Don't encourage your client to phone the prospect unless you can be there for the conversation. Not only do you want the opportunity to meet the prospect, you also want to retain as much control over the conversation as possible. That won't be possible if you aren't present for the call. If the prospect can't be reached by phone during your meeting with the client, then switch to writing a letter for your client's signature instead of rescheduling an appointment to try another call. Rescheduling for another try often results in wasting time and frustrating your client.

Personal Invitation to Prospect by Client for Lunch with the Three of You

A lunch meeting helps you to get to know the prospect in a social atmosphere where the discussion can be general. Getting to know the prospect as a person should help with your sales approach. This is certainly the most personal and effective method of introduction, but arranging three schedules can be a major headache.

Inviting the Client and Prospect to a Special Event

Inviting your client and the referred prospect to a special event is a great way to promote good feelings and establish new relationships. Events might include a pro baseball game, a round of golf, a special plant tour, or a holiday party. Make sure the event's cost is in line with the value of your product or service. Many a salesperson has lost a client and a prospect because they *overspent* the value of the product. Rather than impressing the client, they raised questions in the client's mind about how badly he or she must have been overcharged.

CLOSING THE REFERRAL ACQUISITION MEETING

Every customer has more referrals to give. Look upon the close of the referral acquisition meeting as the beginning of referral income from your client. Just as you hope for additional sales to your client in the future, you should also look for additional referrals.

As you close the acquisition meeting, tell the client how much you appreciate his or her trust and confidence and that you'll keep him or her fully informed of what happens with each referral. Ask your client's permission to check with him or her from time to time and see if he or she has more referrals for you. Leave a few business cards for him or her to pass along. Remember this is a meeting for referral acquisition only; don't clutter the conversation by discussing the sale or his or her future need for your products. Save those topics for your post-sale meeting(s).

POST-SALE CLIENT MAINTENANCE

Just as you maintain communication with your client after the sale to build the relationship and procure additional sales opportunities, you should build your referral relationship to generate more referrals. No matter how well you and your company performed, if you allow the client to forget about you—he or she will.

Ideally, you should develop a post-sale contact format that allows you to "touch" the client at least seven or eight times a year. Once a month would be ideal. These contacts can include a number of formats, and the most effective programs incorporate several methods. Certainly your contacts may combine several kinds of messages, such as personal greetings, product or service specials that might interest the client, important company or personal announcements, and asking for additional referrals. Effective formats include:

- personal phone calls
- emails and letters

Referral Generation Tip

Give Your Client a Reason to Read Your Communi-cations. Don't send mail or email just to be sending some-thing. When sending a communications to a client or prospect, make sure it contains something of value. Send-ing meaningless communications will simply train your recipient to trash your mailings without reading them.

- monthly or quarterly newsletters

- postcards

- holiday and special occasion cards and gifts

- office drop bys

The three keys to an effective follow-up program are consistency, personal contact, and maintaining interest. Your program must be consistent. A hit-or-miss program where you contact your client three or four times in a row and then allow months to pass is less effective than a consistent flow of contacts over a long period of time. You want to keep your name constantly in his mind, not just on occasion.

The program must be personal. No matter what the format, you must develop a way to maintain an impression of personal communi-cation. Obviously, phone calls are personal and letters can be easily personalized. With a little more effort, even postcards, emails, and newsletters can be personalized. This is a personal communication from you to your client, designed to keep your name (not your com-pany's name) in front of him or her.

And the program must keep your client's interest. If you don't provide something of interest, the client will learn to ignore your communication. A contact program isn't something to just throw together. You must train your clients to read your letters, take your phone calls, study your newsletters, and look at your postcards by making sure each communication has some benefit for them; otherwise it goes straight into the trash. Most mass mail is designed with the expectation that it won't be read by the average recipient. It's designed to communicate one thing no matter how quickly the card gets tossed from the mail pile into the trash—a company name. However, your personal "mass mail" can be designed so your clients will recognize value in reading it—if you take the time and effort to make it beneficial to them.

It isn't unreasonable to expect three or four additional referrals a year from each of your past clients. Some salespeople can realistically anticipate several hundred referrals a year from past customers, simply because they did a quality job and then religiously maintained contact over the years. I've had my auto insurance with the same company and agent for over 20 years. I haven't spoken to the agent or his staff in over 5 years. But every month I will get at least one "personal" communication from him, in the form of a birthday or holiday card, a quarterly newsletter, an announcement postcard of some type, or my annual "review." I probably refer two to three people a year to him. Why? Because he keeps his name in front of me. Since I haven't had a claim in 20 years and haven't spoken to his staff in over 5 years, I can't honestly say he provides superior customer service—I haven't had a reason to find out. But he keeps his name in front of me, and because of that he gets the opportunity to sell two or three people I know every year. What do these referrals mean to him in terms of income? I have no idea. But over 20 years I've probably referred 50 to 60 potential clients. If half of his client base does the same, he's making a lot of money by investing only a little effort and expense.

At www.pwwrreferrals.com you'll find an extensive list of companies who can help you create your email, newsletter, postcard, and other printed campaigns, as well as help you establish and maintain your client and prospect mailing lists. These links will also provide ideas about creating successful campaigns that will keep your customers interested.

PERSONAL INVENTORY

Make a list of all past clients you can approach and ask for referrals:

_____

_____

_____

_____

What methods do you currently use to maintain contact with your past clients?

_____

_____

_____

What methods can you implement quickly, effectively, and within a reasonable budget?

_____

_____

CHAPTER 9

Contacting the Referred Prospect

Your initial contact with the referred prospect sets the tone for a new salesman-client relationship. This contact should be partly based on what kind of relationship the prospect has with your client. The prospect-client relationship usually falls into one of four categories: family, friend, coworker/past coworker, or acquaintance. Occasionally you'll receive a referral from a client to someone he only knows by reputation.

KNOW YOUR TRUST LEVEL BEFORE YOU CONTACT THE PROSPECT

No matter what the relationship, you must first find out if your new prospect respects the referrer's judgment. Sometimes you'll uncover enough information during the referral acquisition to answer this question. If the prospect respects the referrer's opinion, you can use your client's name without hesitation. Give the prospect a full account of your dealings with your client and encourage him to talk to the client. More than likely the prospect won't even call the client; the fact that someone he respects has referred you will be enough. You're building a relationship based on the prospect's trust of the referrer.

On the opposite end of the spectrum is a prospect who doesn't respect your client's opinion. In such a case, you should take care how and when you use your client's name. Using your client's name to gain entrance to the prospect may be as far as you want to go in discussing your sale and relationship to the client. You won't have the advantage of preestablished trust with the prospect, but at least you've gained access to him or her. Your starting position with this prospect will range from slightly negative to strongly negative, based on his or her opinion of your client.

You may want to encourage the prospect to call the referrer and get a firsthand account of his or her experience with you, your company, and your product. Since you know the prospect doesn't hold your client in high regard, it's important to give him or her a chance to ask specific questions about your performance. Then he or she can form his

Referral Generation Tip

Work Your Best Referrals First. Prioritize each referral you receive from a client and work the strongest referrals first. Don't allow a hot, high-quality referral to turn cold by neglect.

or her own opinion based on the facts rather than your client's name. The more evidence you provide, the sooner you can build credibility with the prospect.

The final category of prospects has a neutral opinion of your client. Often these are casual acquaintances from organizations the client belongs to, or past business associates with whom he or she only had casual contact. These prospects usually respond positively to a meeting based on the client's referral, but you'll have to move your relationship from neutral to a positive position. You can gain more trust by encouraging this prospect to call your client and ask detailed questions about your produce or service. The more personal you make the referral, the more quickly you gain your prospect's trust.

THE INITIAL PROSPECT CONTACT

Each of the contact methods discussed in Chapter 8 indicates how to make your initial contact.

1. Referred by name and phone number: This is usually the least effective method of referral contact and is only slightly better than a cold call, depending upon the strength of the relationship between the prospect and the referrer. Using the name of someone the prospect knows should at least get you past the gatekeeper. However, if the referrer has a strong relationship with your new prospect, this method of contact can be highly effective. Your call to the prospect may be little more than a personal introduction, a brief statement of what you do, why your client referred you, and a request for a brief meeting. If the relationship is weak, you may have to ask for a meeting several times before the prospect agrees.

With a weak relationship between prospect and client, you'll need a stronger referral format. In this case, it's best to have your client call the prospect while you're in his or her office. The next best scenario is a personal letter from the client, written by you, with his or her signature. If your efforts to upgrade the contact format fail, then go ahead and make the contact with a phone call, but be aware that your starting point with the prospect is similar to a warm call, at best. Be prepared to make a full cold-call presentation, using your client's name and referral with force. Don't apologize for calling, and speak with a strong, self-assured voice. Even though you're prepared to make the full presentation, begin as though you only need your client's name and referral. Then, if need be, fall back to a full-presentation format. Assume your client's name and referral are strong enough to make the close, but be mentally prepared to treat the call as a cold call if necessary.

Whether the relationship between prospect and referrer is strong or weak, thoroughly review your notes from the referral acquisition meeting. When you talk with the prospect, you should have all of the information about him or her and his or her company on the tip of your tongue. Your phone call is the prospect's initial impression of you and your company, and you should make the best possible impression. Many a referral has been muffed by a salesperson who didn't review his or her notes and made inaccurate comments about the prospect or his or her company.

2. Email from client to prospect: Avoid this contact format if at all possible. Emails are quickly deleted, and the prospect will forget he or she ever heard of you or your company. If your client insists on sending an email, assume the prospect won't remember your name, what you do, or why you're calling. In other words, treat your initial phone call as a cold call and expect nothing from the email your client sent the prospect.

3. Personal letter from client to prospect written by client: This format will greatly increase the percentage of prospects who will set appointments with you. It's effective even with a weak relationship between prospect and client. Before calling the prospect you'll need to know when your client sent the letter and whether the letter was sent to the prospect's home or office. It's best if the client gives the letters to you so you can mail them yourself, giving you more control over the process. Stagger the mailings and follow-up on one or two letters per day. For example, if your client gives you five referral letters, send two on one day and plan to follow up with these prospects 3 or 4 days later. Two or three days after mailing the first two letters, send out two more, and then mail the final letter a few days later. This gives you plenty of time to follow up with each prospect and helps prevent cramming several initial prospect meetings into a single week.

During your initial call to the prospect, assume he or she received and read the client's letter and is expecting your call. Briefly introduce yourself, review your product or service and what you did for the referring client, and ask for an appointment. Since you have a stronger referral, assume you'll get a close on the appointment. Be prepared for objections, but the most effective approach after a personal letter is to assume the prospect has a basic understanding of what you do, is interested, and wants to meet you. Close for an appointment with confidence and without going into great detail about what you do.

4. Personal letter from client to prospect written by you with your client's signature: The best letter format is for you to take a few pieces of your client's stationary and write letters for him or her.

133

You know your product and service better than anyone, so you can write the most effective letter to prospects. This frees your client from the task of writing letters and ensures they're written in a timely fashion. Don't overstate your accomplishments with your client. Write directly, truthfully, and without excessive praise of yourself and your company. You should customize the letter with specific information about the prospect and his or her company, and also specify a time and date when you'll call the prospect (since you're in charge of mailing the letter). Be sure you call exactly as promised, or you'll ruin your credibility with the prospect before you even talk to him or her. Remember, you've relied on your client's relationship with the prospect to build trust, so you can't afford to do anything—even something as small as missing a phone call—that will undermine this referral.

On page 135 is a referral letter written on my behalf by one of my management consulting clients. The next page contains the version of the letter I wrote for my client to sign. I believe my version is more personal, specific to the prospect's needs, and much more effective. All statements in my version of the letter came from the client during our referral acquisition meeting.

5. Personal phone call from client to prospect: Having your client call the prospect during the referral acquisition meeting guarantees an appointment. It's difficult for a prospect to decline a meeting when the client has him or her on the phone. Because a personal call like this is so unusual, the prospect will assume there's something different about you. I've asked hundreds of clients, prospects, and business executives how many times they had received a personal phone call of recommendation from a friend, colleague, or acquaintance. Only a handful said they'd ever received such a call. You'll make a strong impression because the event is so rare. Who would take the

Carlson Technologies

123 Broad Street
Austin, Texas 78035

November 9, 2004

Thomas Drake
Drake and Sons
5555 Monitor Ave
Austin, Texas

Dear Tom,

I want to introduce you to Paul McCord of McCord and Associates. Paul has been helping me work through some of the issues we've had in our sales and marketing departments and the solutions he has developed for our company are proving to be of great value for us.

Since you had mentioned a while back that you are not happy with the compensation plan you have for your sales team, I think you might find it to be worth your while to talk with Paul to see if he might be able to help you as he did us.

Sincerely,

Hal Carlson

Carlson Technologies
123 Broad Street
Austin, Texas 78035

November 9, 2004

Thomas Drake
Drake and Sons
5555 Monitor Ave
Austin, Texas

Dear Tom,

If you will recall our conversation of a few months ago, I had mentioned we were experiencing a decline in sales while our cost of sales were increasing. At the time I couldn't figure out what the problem was since we were doing the same things we had been doing in the past, but for some reason, things seemed to getting out of control. I finally decided to call in an expert to analyze the situation and give us a hand at getting things turned around.

Paul McCord with McCord and Associates out of Houston has made a significant impact in a short period of time. By implementing Paul's recommendations we have already experienced a reversal of our decline in sales, we've gotten a grip on our cost of sales, and have made improvements to our customer service department as well. Whereas we were projecting a decline of almost 10% in sales for next year, we are now projecting a 12-14% increase.

You mentioned that you are not happy with the compensation and incentive plan your company has for your sales force and that you are seriously thinking of expanding into a couple of new markets but are concerned about the development costs. I think, based on my experience, that it would be well worth your time to sit down with Paul for a brief discussion. His knowledge and experience is really helping us and I believe he could be of value to you also.

I've asked Paul to give you a call Monday morning at 7:30. I thought this would give you time for a brief discussion before your crew gets in and your day starts to become hectic.

Sincerely,

time and effort to make such a call unless they were totally sold on the salesperson and his or her product? Besides gaining an appointment, the personal call referral helps you go into that first meeting with the attitude that you're there to help the prospect, not sell him or her. You assume the position of a consultant who's ready to help solve a problem, exactly as you did for the prospect's friend. You aren't just a salesperson trying to land a big sale; you enter the new relationship from a position of strength.

6. Personal invitation from client to prospect to lunch or an event: The strongest referral you can receive is when your client invites the prospect to meet you for lunch or another social event. Not only do you have an impressive commitment from your client to make a personal call to the prospect, you have at least 45 minutes to spend with the prospect—and your client will act as your co-salesperson. You don't have to sell; your client will sell for you, letting you assume the position of expert consultant. If you could manage to use this format for every referral you receive, your closing ratio would be well above 90%. Unfortunately, this format is hard to develop with clients. Most people only have time to meet one or two referrals for lunch. Save this approach for your best referral prospects. Work to get each client to invite one prospect to lunch—and make sure it's the best of his or her referrals. Don't ask a client to waste his or her time (and your money) on a weak prospect.

The stronger the referral method you use, the better your chance of setting an initial meeting with the prospect. Likewise, the stronger the relationship is between your client and the prospect, the better your chances of making a sale. Evaluate your referrals based on these two criteria and contact your strongest prospects first. If you start with your strong referrals and have success, you'll feel less pressure when

137

contacting weaker prospects. If you begin by calling your weakest prospects and fail, you'll feel pressure to succeed as you speak with your best prospects—and often the stress and pressure of feeling you must succeed will come through in your voice, making you sound desperate. Manage your system so you eliminate as much stress and pressure as possible. You want your voice to reflect the confidence success brings, not the desperation brought on by stress and failure.

Go to www.pwwrreferrals.com for additional information on how to effectively contact your referred prospects, including examples of introductory statements, overcoming objections, and how to use your client's name and the services you provided for your client.

CHAPTER **10**

The Next Generation of Referrals

At some point you'll be challenged to keep your referral business growing. As you convert a sales business to a referral-based business, you will be busy dealing with open orders and have less time to contact referred prospects. Converting from a marketing business to a primarily sales business may cause a great deal of pain and frustration unless you anticipate problems and put systems in place *before* you're overwhelmed by time-consuming selling and communication issues. For many salespeople, establishing a sales business is more difficult and frustrating than the marketing business they're converting from. Much of the frustration arises from having to shift their efforts to more client-oriented functions. Another source of frustration comes from losing the freedom and spontaneity they had when their focus was primarily on prospecting. They must become far more disciplined and focused than their previous business required.

Depending on how your company supports your sales efforts, you may find yourself losing control of time and—if you aren't careful—neglecting your customers. You'll wake up one morning and discover the day is filled with monitoring orders, contacting customers about pending sales, and working with the accounting office, customer service, and other departments. You'll be tempted to put off making referral prospect calls until things slow down a bit. A day or two becomes a week or two. The next thing you know, you look at your pipeline and realize almost all your sales have closed and you have nothing to take their place—but you have a stack of referral letters to send out. Too late!

In most industries, it takes a certain amount of time from initial contact with a new prospect (even a referred prospect) until you close the sale. Many salespeople experience dreaded ups and downs; they close a fair amount of business one month, and then suffer through 1 or 2 thin months while they refill the pipeline. You must be proactive and develop a method that lets you maintain your selling activity while monitoring and closing an active pipeline of business.

One of the quickest ways to organize your work is to designate two times during the day when you return phone calls and answer emails. Establish a morning and an afternoon time period for these activities. Publish these times on your office and mobile phone voice mails, attach them to your email signatures, and make sure your clients, coworkers, and prospects know when you'll return their calls and emails. And then stick to the times religiously, except for true emergencies. You can waste a great deal of time each day by constantly answering the phone and emails. Most of these communications will be distractions rather than important issues. If you're in a business where you must be available throughout the day for emergencies from

Referral Generation Tip

Keep a Database of Each Client's Referrals. Keeping a database of each client's referrals, the referred customer's referrals, and so on, will quickly demonstrate the power of referrals and give you tremendous encouragement—spurring you on to even more referrals and sales. This will give you a family tree to refer to as you thank your clients. They will appreciate knowing you've tracked their contributions to your business.

customers or departments within your company, acquire a second mobile phone and only give that number to people who might need to reach you immediately. Let them know that number is for true emergencies only.

Save time by creating a series of email templates you can quickly and easily customize for each client. Create an email for each of the common communications you have with customers, prospects, and internal company issues. All you need do is fill in the recipient's name and a little specific information on the issue. If designed correctly, these emails can be sent in just a few seconds. For example, if you regularly send messages informing clients their product will be shipped as scheduled, create an email template such as, "Dear _____, Just wanted to let you know the delivery scheduled for _____ is all set. Thanks! (Salesperson)."

Another effective timesaver is to establish a set time each week when you'll communicate with all of your customers to update them on the status of their orders, answer questions, and resolve minor issues. Of course, your clients will contact you if they have issues before

Referral Generation Tip

Don't Let Yourself Forget. As your business grows, so do your contact commitments. Scheduled phone calls, meetings, and other promises become harder and harder to remember. Set each scheduled activity on your Client Relationship Management program or other contact management software to automatically remind you each morning with a pop-up of your promised activities. Don't shut down your computer at the end of the day until you have checked each item as either completed or rescheduled.

the scheduled call, but a weekly phone call should be enough for most customers. By placing these calls all on one day, you can more easily clear your schedule for other activities.

It's vitally important to set aside a fixed amount of time each day or week to follow up on referrals. A sales business cannot survive unless you continually feed new prospects and customers into the pipeline. Unfortunately, referrals don't automatically become customers. Depending on how long it takes from your first meeting to consummating a sale, you may have dozens of prospects in your files at any time, all in various stages of being sold. Each of these prospects requires time and effort to turn them into clients. Setting aside a specified time each day or week to cultivate these prospects will help guarantee your pipeline stays full.

Setting aside time may not be enough to solve the management problems created by your referral business. Obtaining a good Client Relationship Management (CRM) program can significantly increase your time management ability. This program will help you keep each

Referral Generation Tip

"Refer" Backward to Your Referral Source. Once you've completed a successful sale with a referred customer, ask him or her to send a thank you note back to the person who referred you. Positive feedback from someone he or she referred will encourage customers to continue giving you referrals.

prospect's and client's information in order and allow you to schedule tasks, appointments, and calls that pop up as automatic reminders.

Even this may not be enough. You may need to develop a prospect management system that rates each of your prospects according to a set of guidelines you establish. For example, I rate each of my prospects on a scale from A to D. Each letter represents the potential for generating a sale within a given time frame. In my system, I rate prospects as A if I believe they'll make a purchase decision within 30 days; B-rated prospects are expected to make a purchase decision within 60 days; C prospects are expected to make a decision within 120 days; and D prospects are more long-term. I have subcategories within each category. Prospects with a 1 represent an expected sale over $30,000; prospects with a 2 fall between $10,000 and $29,999; and prospects with a 3 are less than $10,000. Consequently, my ratings will be A-1 through D-3. I weigh each task based on the prospect's rating.

This rating system doesn't mean I can ignore things I've committed to do for prospects in the C and D categories, or those in the number 3 subcategory. It simply means that if I have conflicting tasks, I can prioritize who comes first. If I have to eliminate a few prospects because I can't handle the business, I have a way to determine who can be eliminated. The unfortunate reality is, I must spend my immediate time and energy on an A-2 prospect or a B-1 prospect, rather than a D-2 prospect who may not be ready to purchase for up to 8 months. If the D-2 prospect is demanding a great deal of my time, I can't afford to give up an immediate sure thing for a long-term possibility.

If you're an independent salesperson, such as a realtor, mortgage loan officer, or financial planner, as your sales volume expands you should consider delegating mundane tasks to an assistant. A competent assistant will help you grow your business by as much as three to four times what you could handle by yourself, while substantially improving customer service. Hiring an assistant is a major step for any salesperson. The most obvious consideration when contemplating this step is how the person will be paid and who will be responsible for the salary. In most cases, you will be responsible for hiring, training, and paying the assistant—at least until your volume justifies the company paying all or a portion of your assistant's salary. Hiring an assistant part-time and allowing him or her to grow into the job while you grow your business has been a successful formula for many salespeople.

Carefully monitor your pipeline and prospect growth and hire an assistant before you actually need one. You'll need time to train and integrate this person into your business, and if you wait until you desperately need help, you'll find it difficult to maintain customer service and train your assistant at the same time. Anticipate a reduction in your personal income for a short period of time once you hire the assistant, since you'll be paying his or her salary without seeing enough immediate new business to make up for it. Once your assistant is up to speed with the job—usually within 60 to 90 days—focus on cre-

146

ating new business. This will help you justify your new hire and take advantage of the extra time you've gained.

At www.pwwrreferrals.com you will find a full discussion of hiring and training an assistant as well as outlines of a number of assistant-payment plans that have worked for salespeople in various industries.

PERSONAL INVENTORY

Where are you wasting time in your selling business?

_____

_____

_____

_____

What is your prospect rating system and what criteria do you use to determine each prospect's status?

_____

_____

_____

What time-saving and customer service improvement systems do you currently have in place?

_____

_____

What systems can you employ that you are not currently using?

_____

_____

CHAPTER **11**

What If
They Don't
Buy?

Up to this point we've discussed how you can generate referrals from clients and customers, and this is how you'll obtain most of your referred prospects. However, prospects who choose not to purchase from you may also provide quality referrals. They won't give you a large number of referrals, and the strength of most of these referrals will be relatively weak, since they can't give personal testimonials about your product. Still, it's better than cold calls.

To request referrals from prospects that didn't purchase, employ an abbreviated form of the referral process you use with clients. In most cases you'll acquire a few names and phone numbers of people your prospect believes can use your product. It usually isn't realistic to expect a prospect to call or write to someone on your behalf.

Since you've made a standard approach to the nonpurchasing prospect, he or she should be prepared for your referral request. By the time he or she reaches the decision-making point, he or she has a good grasp of how you work, how professional you are, the potential capabilities of your product or service, and a feel for your company. If you performed your sales job properly to this point, you should be able to request the names and phone numbers of two or three people. This is usually a reasonable request, depending on why the prospect didn't purchase.

Before asking for referrals, you must know why the prospect decided not to follow through with the sale. If his or her reasons don't relate negatively to you, your company, or your product and you've maintained a professional selling process, you stand an excellent chance of getting referrals. However, if the prospect has issues with you, your company, or your product, don't expect to acquire referrals until you uncover and resolve those problems. The one exception is if the prospect objects to the price. Assuming your pricing is competitive, it shouldn't prevent a prospect from referring you to another prospect.

Once you receive the names and phone numbers of referred parties, call them and use your prospect's name as your introduction. These referrals are most useful for generating names and helping you get the opportunity to talk with people. Conversion ratios to sales fall on the low side, but the referral is easy to get and is your form of payment for the time and effort you invested in a nonsale.

CHAPTER **12**

Creating
Referral
Partnerships

More than likely you sell a product or service through which you can mine other ancillary sources for new prospects. Depending upon your industry, these nonclient prospect sources may become a primary tool for customer generation. For example, if you're in the mortgage industry, your primary sources of new clients may come from realtors, builders, financial planners, and others who would have a regular need to refer a customer to a mortgage firm. If you sell automobiles, your sources might include insurance agents and adjusters, or owners of paint shops, body shops, or repair shops whose customers may be getting a car ready to trade. An insurance agent may seek referrals from mortgage loan officers, auto salespeople, and realtors, among others.

Even people we don't think of as salespeople must develop their businesses through referrals. Take, for instance, a cardiologist who only works with patients referred from other physicians. He must sell his noncardiologist peers on referring their patients to him, and he must do this through some format—probably personal networking, or simply on the strength of his reputation.

Each of us has a unique set of potential referral sources, depending on our particular product or service, and we all have an opportunity to develop these relationships into long-term partners. If we select our referral partners correctly, we can vault ourselves to amazing levels of production.

Traditionally salespeople have been encouraged to seek "spheres of influence" that can refer business back to them. These spheres of influence could be virtually anyone—family members, friends, business acquaintances, past schoolmates, or a number of other people you might meet. The basic idea is to let them know what you're doing and how they can help you—that is, who they should be referring to you. The sphere of influence concept teaches that if you approach enough of these people who like and respect you, you'll eventually get a significant number of referrals. The idea is the same as the numbers concept in selling—see enough people and you will sell. Here, the idea is that if you talk to enough potential business referrers, you'll get referrals.

Although the scatter gun approach to creating a sphere of influence has worked for salespeople for decades, there's a better way to create referral business. This method works especially well with salespeople and businesses that complement your products or services.

REFERRAL SOURCES OR REFERRAL PARTNERS?

The deadliest sin a salesperson can commit when he or she thinks about developing a sphere of influence referral base is to view the prospective referral sources as just that—sources of referrals. Potential referral sources aren't in the market to generate business for you, nor are they looking for some place to send referrals. Your potential referral sources are in business to make money. Like you, they're looking for new clients. You share the same needs and desires—to connect with someone who can provide referrals.

If you want to connect with a referral source who'll generate a steady stream of referrals, you will need to establish a significant, long-term relationship. Looking upon a potential referral source as a partner changes the way you approach and work with him or her, and it may also change who you consider as a potential referral source.

Let me give examples from the mortgage industry and two loan officers I've known. One mortgage loan officer, David, was fairly new to the industry. During his training he was exhorted to develop realtors and builders into referral sources. He worked diligently for months, contacting at least one new realtor or builder per day. He would meet them at networking events, drop into their offices, and attend industry meetings. He was careful to always have a pocket full of business cards, a smile, and a firm handshake. He had a personal infomercial about himself and his company down pat: "I'm great and I'll work hard for you and your clients. My company has great rates; we can close your hard loans just as well as we can close your easy loans. We close your loans quickly. We have hundreds of programs. Our fees are among the lowest in the area, and I'm available 24 hours a day, 7 days a week."

157

But David was indiscriminate in who he approached. He spent as much time pursuing new realtors who'd never sold a home as he did with highly experienced realtors and successful builders—more, in fact. He spent little time with successful people because he'd been told they already had relationships with loan officers and, consequently, wouldn't be willing to talk with him. He didn't want to waste time pursuing dead ends.

David was dogged in looking for referrals. Unfortunately, his approach was nothing even the new realtors hadn't already heard a thousand times. A few of the realtors he spoke with were receptive to his message, but most were either noncommittal or brushed him off.

After 4 months of hard work, David had developed five realtors into what he believed were his referral base. All had less than 2 years experience in the business, and three had less than 1 year. On average, they closed about five contracts a year, including both listings and sales. If each realtor referred him 40% of their business, he'd generate less than one referral a month. Of course, he had over 70 other realtors he'd met and could continue to develop, but he wouldn't be in business long enough to develop them at the rate he was going.

Janice, like David, was new to the mortgage industry when she joined the company a few weeks after David. In some respects Janice was "behind" David because she'd never sold a product or service before joining the company, whereas David had several years of sales experience behind him. But Janice excelled where David failed because of her ability to develop key referral partners. Her approach to potential referral sources was completely different than David's method. Janice didn't look at realtors as simply potential referral sources to be exploited, but rather as potential business partners with whom she could develop a long-term, profitable business. Her desire was to develop a mutually beneficial partnership with a select group of realtors, where each saw their success bound with the other.

Because Janice wanted to become partners with a small group of realtors, she was selective about whom she approached. She researched a large number of potential partners throughout the city and narrowed the list to several dozen successful realtors who seemed to specialize in selling properties rather than listing property. She then began her hunt for partners.

Unlike David, Janice approached her potential referral partners with ideas they hadn't often heard. She let them know immediately she wanted not a referral source, but a partner. She advocated shared advertising and marketing; she suggested ways they could combine their expertise to present seminars and client appreciation events; she shared with the realtor her belief that it was her duty to refer customers to the realtors, as well as the realtor's duty to refer to her. Janice suggested they consult with a professional design company to create marketing pieces they could both use.

Over a period of roughly 4 months, Janice met with 39 potential partners. During the course of this period she developed 7 of them into partners. These 7 realtors (actually 11, as 4 were teams of two experienced realtors) had an average of 9 years experience in the business and an average annual volume of over $4,000,000 in sales. These 7 realtors had a combined 167 closings the previous year. If Janice captured 40% of their business, she would average a closing of 5½ loans per month. That volume wouldn't make her a superstar, but would certainly ensure she'd be making about $100,000 per year. And she was still trying to develop partnerships with several of the agents she contacted during her initial prospecting. Plus, she still had several hundred prospective realtors to qualify and contact.

Janice continued to use the partnering method. After almost 3 years in the mortgage business, she had over 20 realtor partners. She closed an average of 17 loans per month with an annual income of over $270,000. A rookie no longer, Janice is one of the top producers in her office. She doesn't fret about whether she'll meet her numbers for the coming month. She doesn't worry about whether she'll be able to pay her bills. She doesn't worry about whether she'll be in business at the end of the year. She knows where she's going and how she's going to get there—because she has over 20 successful business partners working to make sure she's just as successful as they are.

Partnering with a potential sphere of influence is time consuming, requires a commitment on your part, and may require some financial investment. But the rewards you gain through number and quality of referrals, the loyalty of the other party, and the satisfaction and security of developing a long-term business will far exceed your investment of time and dollars.

WHO IS A POTENTIAL PARTNER?

As you consider creating partnerships with people whose products and services compliment your sales activity, focus on identifying potential partners who will enhance your credibility and can potentially provide a steady supply of quality prospects. Of course, these are the most difficult potential partners to interest in developing a partnership.

Who Is a Potential Partner?

The tendency, particularly with relatively new salespeople, is to focus on salespeople and companies you feel comfortable approaching. Since human nature is such that we feel most comfortable with others who are similar to ourselves, the temptation is to approach others with the same level of knowledge and experience. In order to develop a referral partner network that will quickly enhance your stature in your industry and expand your sales volume, you need to leave your safety zone. Don't just approach people who are nonthreatening. Focus on building relationships with the most successful people you can find.

If you are willing to invest the time and energy necessary, partnering offers an exceptional opportunity to take several giant steps forward in establishing your image and reputation within your potential customer base by piggybacking on your new partner's image and reputation. Obviously, this implies that your new partner must already have the image and reputation you are seeking for yourself.

How do you find these people? Start by closely examining your products and services, your potential customer base, and your sales process.

What products or services compliment your products and services? For example, if you sell communications equipment to mid- to large-size firms, think about other equipment or services these companies use that aren't supplied by your company. If you wholesale mutual funds to NASD broker/dealer firms, what noncompetitive products do other salespeople offer to these firms? If you sell high-end residential remodeling, what other products might homeowners consider when they decide to spend $65,000 to have their kitchen remodeled?

List at least eight complimentary products or services that compliment the products you sell:

1. _____

2. _____

3. _____

4. _____

5. _____

6. _____

7. _____

8. _____

After completing your list, consider which salespeople and firms from each of these categories have the strongest image and reputation in your area. Consider which salespeople you run across most often, which ones you hear the most positive feedback about, and who seems to have the strongest business. If you have difficulty developing a list, enlist clients and prospects by asking them which of the products and services from your list they use and who their vendors are. Also ask who their salespeople are—and specifically why they chose those products, services, vendors, and salespeople. Another option is to examine membership lists of the organizations and associations for companies that manufacture or sell the products on your list.

Depending on the size of your selling territory, within a short time you should have a list of at least several dozen—and possibly hundreds—of companies and salespeople for each of the products and services on your list. Prioritize your list of potential partners from strongest to weakest according to their reputation, image, and sales volume. Since the list consists of only strong companies and salespeople with the reputation, image, and volume that interest you, the variance from the strongest prospect to the weakest probably won't be great.

YOUR PARTNERING PROPOSITION

With list in hand, prepare to make contact with your prospective partners by developing your partnering proposition. Your partnering proposition must present a win/win/win package: Your prospective partner must find it to his or her advantage to work with you, and he or she must determine that the partnership will benefit both your customers. The package you develop must also provide significant benefits to you and your company. Generally, your partnering proposition will include at least these items, which are discussed in the following paragraphs.

Marketing Considerations

Any proposed partnership with your potential referral source should provide a plan for coordinated marketing. This certainly doesn't mean you'll create an expensive, elaborate campaign, but there should be some joint marketing to mutual prospects.

Such a campaign may be no more elaborate than a couple of joint fliers or email solicitations; it should be as expansive and expensive as both parties can afford. The object of the campaign is to: (a) reach new potential prospects, and (b) create opportunities for joint or piggy-back sales.

Combining prospect lists with your new partner will create a larger pool of prospects for both of you. One of the primary reasons you want to team with companies and salespeople with superior images and reputations is so your image and reputation will become paired with theirs. As a partner with joint marketing to their prospect list, you'll have your information presented to prospects in a favorable manner—and many of these prospects may be people and companies you couldn't reach otherwise, based only on your own merits.

Simply suggesting a joint marketing campaign probably won't play well with a prospective partner unless you also present a compelling argument showing how partnering and joining marketing forces will benefit him or her. Although you don't need to present a fully developed idea, you must be ready to discuss what type of joint marketing you believe will be beneficial, how you think it will be beneficial, and what the specific results for the business will be—both short-term and long-term.

When considering a joint marketing campaign, examine in detail how your prospective partner currently markets. What marketing tools does he or she use? Assuming you have limited financial means to dedicate to a program, what media does he or she use that will adapt to joint marketing? Is there a consistent theme or look to each type of medium he or she uses? How professional does it appear? How expensive?

Your answers to these questions won't create a marketing campaign for you, but they will indicate what direction to go in. If your prospective partner uses expensive, multipage brochures but doesn't use fliers, it will be difficult to interest him or her in creating a flier for a joint marketing campaign. Either he or she doesn't believe fliers work or he or she believes fliers are inconsistent with his or her image. (Remember, you may disagree with his or her beliefs, but you must understand what he or she believes and either sell him or her on your way of thinking or accept his or her concepts and work within his or her framework.) Perhaps he or she has concluded that his or her product and/or service requires a more detailed, sophisticated approach than a flier can accomplish. If your prospective partner consistently uses humor in marketing, you will need to consider incorporating humor into your joint marketing. If all of his or her marketing highlights price, understand that price will probably need to be a major part of your joint marketing.

Keep in mind that since this partnership is between you and a fellow salesperson, your combined marketing won't be as expensive as the other person's corporate advertising, but you still need to be aware that his or her company may have a marketing program that's working effectively. If so, he or she will probably want to mimic that program as much as possible—at least as much as the budget will allow.

When constructing your joint marketing, quality and presentation are important. You're better off having only a couple of quality fliers instead of trying to cover too many bases and ending up with something that will embarrass both of you.

Sales Considerations

Of course, the purpose for the partnership and joint marketing is to create new business for each of you. When approaching a prospective partner with a partnership proposition, you need to emphasize how he or she will benefit through additional business. That business should come from two sources: new prospects he or she can reach and influence through your prospect list and new or additional sales that arise from his or her own prospect list due to piggybacking on your product or service.

Just as with developing a joint marketing program plan, your sales benefit plan doesn't need to be a fully developed, exact projection of the new business your proposed partner can expect. But you must be prepared with ideas of how the partnership will impact his or her sales volume and profitability—and where those additional sales will come from.

Since you had the opportunity to research his or her company while examining its marketing materials, you should have a good idea of its target prospect and an approximate idea of its typical sales size. Armed with this information, you can examine your client and prospect list to decide how many potential new qualified prospects you can provide for your partner. Make a projection as to how much potential business this will represent. The potential new customers from your list will consist of customers your partner may add to his or her list, plus his or her existing customers who may increase their orders for his or her products. Your analysis of potential new business for your proposed partner should be on the conservative side because you can expect him or her to question how you came up with your figures and why you believe they're realistic. If you aren't credible, he or she will quickly lose interest. By presenting a cohesive, workable, well-thought-out plan to increase your potential partner's business, you prove yourself a serious, knowledgeable professional. The fact that you understand his or her business and how working with you can realistically increase his or her sales volume will force him or her to take you seriously—after all, if he or she doesn't listen, he or she knows the competition probably will.

While constructing a sales plan for your proposed partner, you must also examine the potential for your own sales volume. A one-way program that enhances your new partner but doesn't provide you with sales growth isn't your goal. As you describe the advantages he or she can expect from this program to your potential partner, you also need to explain how the program will benefit you. Just as you must gain agreement with a client regarding what constitutes a quality job, there must be agreement from each party regarding the goals and objectives of the partnership. Not everyone is a team player. If you can't get the prospect to agree he or she will work on your behalf (just as you will be working on his or hers), then you need to move on to the next prospect on your list.

Pricing and Service Considerations

As you create a marketing and sales plan, you need to consider how the combined efforts of your two companies can benefit your common customers. Are there ways that combining your products and services can lead to discounts, upgrades, or other considerations that will benefit your customers—and help both partners? How does combining your products and expertise make the process more convenient for the customer? Will these considerations increase sales volume for both companies? Will they open new sales avenues or create sales advantages the competition doesn't have?

Your proposal to your prospective partner should indicate possible areas where a joint sale will create added value for the customer, your partner, and yourself. Although the majority of your sales won't include the referral partner, you must find ways to create value for him or her—and that will most likely occur through constructing joint sale/piggyback opportunities. A joint sale or piggyback selling opportunity works best when the customer can easily recognize the added value he or she receives by dealing with both partners.

SELLING THE PARTNERSHIP PROPOSITION

Once you've researched potential partners and created a customized partnership proposal for a particular prospect, it's time to begin the process of selling your concept to your prospective partner.

Before contacting any prospects, take inventory of yourself and your company. By now, your prospect list contains only salespeople working for companies with the image, reputation, and level of business you want to attain. This should be the cream of the crop of companies and salespeople in your area who sell products and services that complement your products. Before you contact these salespeople, take time to examine your own company's image and reputation. Do you personally have the image and reputation these salespeople will want to be associated with? Does your company? If you or your company have image or reputation issues, can they be overcome? If you or your company haven't been in business long, then you probably won't have a problem in this area. *No* image or reputation is better than a *negative* image or reputation. If you already have a poor image and reputation in the industry, then you need to take time to rehabilitate yourself before you look for partners. If your company has a poor reputation within the industry, you may need to change companies before you approach potential partners. Quality salespeople and companies who've devoted years to developing their image and reputation won't associate with a salesperson or company they believe will create a negative impact with customers. Part of your goal in developing referral partnerships is to enhance your image and reputation by piggybacking off your partner. But trying to rehabilitate an image and reputation through a partnership won't work.

Just because you have a product or service that lends itself to partnering doesn't mean you sell the same way your prospective partner does. If you sell in a different way, you should adjust the way you approach your prospect so that you mimic his or her process. That is, if you have a long process that requires repeated meetings over an extended period of time and your prospective partner's process is short—two or three meetings—then approach your prospect on terms he or she is comfortable with. Use a direct approach where you make a proposal with the intent of solidifying an agreement in a short period of time. If your prospect's process is extended, take a more long-term approach to your sale. Let your prospect determine the level of pressure and the speed with which you pursue him or her.

If you're already acquainted with the prospect (and you may well be, since you probably have customers in common), your approach is easy—just call and invite him or her to lunch. If you don't know your prospect, your approach is the same: an invitation to lunch. But in the second instance, your invitation is based on recognizing his or her reputation. An invitation line that I've found works well is: "Hello, John. My name is Paul McCord, with McCord and Associates. I just wanted to call and congratulate you on having developed such a fine reputation in the industry. Although we haven't met, I've heard a good deal about you and would really like the opportunity to take you to lunch. I believe it's always good to know other fine people in our industry, and even though we sell different products, I'd like to take an hour or so of your time to pick your brain."

I don't think I've ever been turned down using this approach. However, it must be true. The prospect must have a good reputation. He or she must be known in the industry. If you called someone who had a poor reputation or was new in the field, you'd have a suspicious individual on the other end of the line—someone wondering what scam you were trying to pull. Assuming your prospect does have a good reputation and is fairly well known within the industry, appealing to his or her ego while giving a sincere compliment virtually guarantees the opportunity to set an appointment.

During the initial lunch meeting you should be concerned with simply getting to know how the prospect does business. Spend a great deal of time listening and asking questions. This will give you the information you need to prepare your proposal. How does he or she find prospects? With what types of clients does he or she prefer to work? Does he or she prefer selling one particular product or service over another? What does he or she seem to sell—performance, price, service, ease of use, or something else? What is his or her sales cycle? Could you work with this person? How would your clients and prospects react to him or her? Does he or she have a sales process that would combine well with yours? Does it seem likely he or she and the company might be receptive to the idea of joining forces to increase business? Are there areas where combining forces can give a value-added edge to each of you?

From your research of the other company you should have a general idea of the answers to these questions, but each salesperson is different. That's why you need to understand exactly how your prospective partner works. Just because you're talking to a successful, respected salesperson doesn't mean you can work with him or her. You're seeking a long-term relationship with someone with whom you'll be working closely, so you should select people you personally like and can get along with. The lunch meeting is as much an interview as the beginning of a sales process. Hopefully you have several dozen salespeople's names on your prospect list. If so, you shouldn't have to compromise by seeking a relationship with someone with whom you aren't comfortable. If you and your prospect can't work smoothly together, your relationship will be doomed from the start, resulting in a wasted opportunity and wasted time for both of you.

If the opportunity arises during your first meeting, you should certainly raise the subject of a possible joint marketing partnership. If you feel it's better to keep the meeting focused on your prospect, or if you'd have to force the subject into the conversation, then it's better to wait for another meeting.

Whether you introduce the subject during your initial meeting or postpone it to a later time, focus your presentation on how your prospect will benefit from the partnership. Also, as a word of caution, the word *partnership* may in itself be a problem for some prospects. We aren't using the word to mean a formal, legal partnership, but rather an informal joining of forces to create additional business opportunities for each party. If you believe partnership might be an issue, then use another phrase, such as joint prospecting, joint venture, or affiliation.

Once you've made your case and generated interest from your prospective partner, let him or her talk. Allow him or her to voice his or her concerns or issues and answer them as fully and honestly as possible. Be prepared for the most common objections:

- "I'm not sure my sales prospects would be interested in using both our companies."

- "My company won't let me work with other companies to sell."

- "I never share my prospect lists."

- "I don't have time to work with anyone else."

- "I don't believe working with another supplier will benefit me."

As with your other sales, you need to flush out the real objections and address them head-on. Joining forces with complementary products and services has been done for decades. It has proven to be a far more effective way to generate business for both parties than the more popular "sphere of influence" method of generating referrals from nonclients. Customers usually like the convenience of dealing with two companies who know and work well with one another, and whose products and service integrate well. Customers also appreciate it when a professional they know and trust refers them to another professional for a product or service they need. With the exception of a few highly regulated products and services, most companies don't object to their salespeople finding creative ways to market the product—and that includes partnering with a noncompeting product or service to increase sales.

WORKING THE PARTNERSHIP

Working the partnership shouldn't require a significant time commitment from either party once you've created the joint plan and marketing materials. The day-to-day working of the partnership is no more complex than regularly informing each other about sales opportunities and new contacts who may need a joint proposal. You'll also contact one another to follow up on previous referrals and joint sales, and to coordinate your mutual marketing campaigns. For the most part, the partnership consists of selling as usual, while keeping an eye out for business opportunities for your partner.

As with most business relationships, the more quality activity you can direct toward your partner, the more activity you'll receive. As the initiator of the partnership proposal, in most cases you'll have the responsibility of beginning the referral process. Your new partner will reasonably expect you to send a few referrals his or her way before you receive anything in return. Often, your recruited partner will harbor some residual skepticism about the concept and the program. You'll need to convince him or her by demonstrating that the concept will work.

Communication between partners is the key to making a joint marketing and referral partnership work. You should take time out on a regular basis during the week to update each other on prospective sales opportunities and refer existing clients to the other partner. Also allot time to brainstorm how you can create more opportunities that will create a bond and lead to additional business for each partner.

If you multiply this concept by several partnerships, you'll experience a significant increase in sales volume within months.

173

CHAPTER **13**

Networking
for
Referrals

Although clients and prospecting partnerships generate the best and most consistent referrals, developing acquaintances from a number of backgrounds can provide a small but useful supplement to your business. Networking through people who have a large number of contacts they might refer to you can generate extra sales during the course of the year. Creating this sphere of influence may require a substantial time investment—time that might be better spent seeking more profitable and consistent prospecting partnerships. But if either of the following networking formats fits your business plan, working them according to the systems outlined in the following paragraphs will help produce the greatest return on time invested.

Generally, salespeople have opportunities to become involved in two different networking situations: becoming a member of a business, civic, fraternal, service, or specialty interest organization and joining an organized networking function. The differences in intent and style of the two groups are significant, as are the networking methods needed to be successful in each situation.

NETWORKING THROUGH BUSINESS, SERVICE, CIVIC, FRATERNAL, AND INTEREST ORGANIZATIONS

Networking within an organization that has a specific purpose other than offering networking opportunities requires a completely different attitude and far different goals than working with clients or potential prospecting partners. While working with clients for referrals is simply part of the sales process, joining a special interest organization requires you to focus on the organization's goals and objectives—and not simply use the group for business purposes. If you join such an organization just to meet the "right people," your efforts will probably fail.

It isn't uncommon to meet a salesperson who attends a Chamber of Commerce function or a Lions Club meeting in order to meet leaders in their respective fields. He decides that knowing these people could benefit his business. So, he joins, though he has no serious interest in the goals and objectives of the organization. He's highly selective in his participation, usually only showing up for the events he believes his "targets" will attend. He sits on the sidelines. He doesn't become involved by donating his time, money, or skills. He's just a seatfiller whose most obvious trait is his religious attendance to the pre- or postmeeting times when he might be able to mingle with the members he specifically wants to meet. He avoids or only briefly acknowledges members who can't help him generate business.

The other members of the organization will eventually—and often quickly—recognize the single-minded purpose of this new member. And they usually resent it. The men and women who wholeheartedly support the organization won't appreciate being used by someone whose primary goal is to advance his own business.

To successfully network through an organization, you must have a genuine interest in their goals and be willing to commit your time, money, and skills to advancing their objectives. Trying to fake interest doesn't work, because you'll eventually become bored and your participation will wane.

If you join an organization without a genuine interest in the group you will fail because you're seeking a quick return on your investment of time. You expect to attend a couple of meetings and to begin to generate referrals from your targets immediately. Rarely does this happen.

Generally it takes months to develop fellow members of an organization into a referral source. Networking organizations is a long-term commitment with a slow payoff. It isn't uncommon for the first referral to take a year or longer to develop. Why? Just as with client and prospecting partner referrals, networking referrals are based on trust—and it usually takes a while to build trust with members of a organization because the opportunities to interact are few. You only see each other on occasion, and personal conversations are typically limited to a few minutes before and after meetings. Even if you take the initiative and invite a member to lunch, this usually won't happen until you've met the person at a couple of events.

In most organizations, the long-time members have watched many people come and go. They tend to be a bit suspicious of new members until these folks prove themselves by staying involved and participating for some period of time. This is especially true in high-profile organizations. Established members of an organization want some assurance that the new member will be active, not just someone who attends a few meetings and then disappears.

Consequently, when you consider networking through organizations, choose one that genuinely holds your interest. If you can't become fully involved with the group and work on its behalf, find another organization to join.

That doesn't mean you shouldn't analyze the membership of different groups as you consider them. Of course you'll want to join an organization where you have a chance to develop referrals from members. Just seek out organizations in which you have a real interest and the desire to devote your time, money, and energy to their causes.

Once you've selected an organization to join, the next consideration is how to approach fellow members as you meet them. Keep in mind that this isn't a selling situation. Selling should be the last thing on your mind. Your goal over the first few meetings is simply to get to know other members on a personal basis. Naturally, your occupation will come up. When the opportunity arises—probably during your initial conversation—give a brief statement (no more than 30 or 40 words) about what you do for people—not what your title is. Your statement should pinpoint exactly what benefit you deliver to your clients, not what you're called. You should seriously think about this 30 to 40 word "infomercial." You want to communicate what you ac-

Referral Generation Tip

Refine Your Personal Infomercial. Your personal info-mercial is your definition of what you do. Take it seri-ously, because it defines exactly where new acquaintances will place you in their mental business databases. Refine the statement until it says exactly what you want to com-municate.

complish for your customers, not what title you carry. Once you've created the word statement, try it on several people and ask for feed-back. Does your statement communicate exactly what you want to say? As you introduce the infomercial, let the other person inquire about how you accomplish the benefit you provide your customers.

Once you've answered the question regarding how you accom-plish what you do, move the conversation back to learning as much as you can about the other member. This initial meeting period is an op-portunity to evaluate other members and to make a decision about where you want to devote you time and efforts within the organiza-tion. By becoming familiar with as many members as possible, you can determine which ones you'd like to develop friendships—and, hopefully business relationships—with, over the next few months. These are the members you'll position yourself to come in contact with most often. You'll volunteer for committees these people are on and participate in the same activities. Again, you aren't using the or-ganization simply as a business tool, but you *are* using your time and effort within that organization to help build your business. By help-ing the organization while helping yourself, you create a win/win sit-uation for all parties.

181

As you become familiar with the various members, you'll have an opportunity to communicate more information about yourself, your company, and your products or services. But your future referrals won't be built upon these conversations. Rather, your future referrals will be built upon the trust you build with fellow members.

Membership in an organization implies you have a significant interest in the goals and objectives of that organization. Other members may judge you according to the amount of time and responsibility you assume. Connie is a salesperson for one of the largest builders in the country. She's been with her employer for about 5 years and was a low- to middle-of-the-pack producer during her first 3 years. During her second year of employment she joined a national service organization that provides eyeglasses to the needy as one of its major goals. Over a period of 2 years, Connie worked diligently within the group and consistently assumed more responsibility. She was not only dedicated and punctual, but also an excellent organizer. Once committed to a project, she made sure it was completed on time and that the results were superior. She had hoped to generate sales from the relationships she developed in the organization. For the first 2 years she belonged to the group, her business referrals from group members were virtually zero. But she didn't let that dampen her enthusiasm for the group. She worked to accomplish the group's goals, led her committees, and accomplished her projects. And people began noticing. Her third year in the group proved to be her business payoff time. During that year she received referrals that translated into over $80,000 in commissions. Combined with her normal sales activity, these referrals brought her annual income to over $200,000. Her fourth year referrals from the organization were a little higher than the third year referrals.

Granted, Connie was more persistent than most of us would be. But her payoff happened because people in her service club noted how she handled duties and responsibilities within their organization. They projected her trustworthiness, dedication, and commitment onto her professional life. They assumed she acted on her job and took care of her job duties the same way she acted within the group. Consequently, they trusted her with referrals. Did the name and reputation of the builder she worked for help her generate the referrals? Probably. Would she have received some of those referrals even if she hadn't shown dedication and trustworthiness through her actions within the organization? Maybe. But it's strange that she labored for 2 years without receiving a single decent referral, and then in her third and fourth years she began generating a significant number of quality referrals. Could it be attributed to anything other than proving herself to other members of the group and gaining their trust through her work within the organization?

Like generating referrals through clients and prospecting partnerships, this method of referral generation isn't a quick fix. But it does generate high-quality referrals and creates referral sources that are more loyal and more interested in referring potential customers than the traditional glad-handing so many salespeople call networking.

NETWORKING EVENTS

Networking events are becoming more common events and are sponsored by all types of organizations. No longer are Chambers of Commerce, industry associations, and business clubs the only sources of business networking events. Today you'll find business networking events hosted by companies, schools, government agencies, entrepreneurs, and many other groups. Most of these events are free, but some are created by entrepreneurs who charge for the privilege of attending.

Compared to the process of researching and targeting a referral partner, or joining a specific organization where you develop referral sources over a period of time, a networking event is a crapshoot. Unless the event is industry specific, you don't know who might attend. Also, unlike the targeted methods, you'll only have a brief opportunity to make contact with a prospective customer or referral source. Consequently, you must focus on meeting and connecting with as many attendees as possible.

Working a networking event requires planning and discipline. If working these events is your primary method for obtaining customers and referral sources, it will require a substantial commitment of time. Expecting to make more than a handful of quality contacts at any single networking event is unrealistic.

Since most communities have dozens—or even hundreds—of networking events every month, you should gather as much information as possible beforehand about whoever is hosting the event. This will help you know who might attend. In many instances, you can call the organization and talk with the event coordinator. He or she can usually give a broad overview of who has attended in the past. If the event is sponsored by an individual or company that charges a fee to attend, they'll probably have a web site. Most of these for-profit networking events also provide a speaker who gives a brief talk. Although the web site may not list past attendees, it will probably list past and future speakers and their topics. This will give you a good idea of who'll be attending. Be selective and only attend events you believe will attract a large crowd, include many attendees who can help in your business, and are free. Why pay for something when dozens of free opportunities exist?

Once you've selected your event, plan on arriving slightly before the advertised start time and stay through the whole thing. Instead of carrying your standard business card, have a stack of larger-size cards printed on heavy, high-quality stock. A slightly larger card will stand out from the others in a stack. The front of the card should be printed as your standard business card and the back should be blank so you have room to write—you'll need it.

If you can afford it, a better plan is to print a 5×4 or 5×6 inch folded, four-color brochure. Again, the back should be blank. A small brochure will let you give more detail about yourself and your business, is less likely to be discarded, and is an excellent substitute for your business card in most situations. If you choose to use the brochure, make sure the quality and content are first class. If you can't afford to have a quality piece produced, don't try to get by with a cheap imitation.

First impressions are always important, especially at networking events. Networking events allow you to meet a large number of people in a short period of time. Unfortunately, you don't have a great deal of time to interact with any single person, nor will you have the opportunity to undo a bad first impression. First impressions are based on looks and—as the phrase indicates—general impression. Do you look professional? Do you act professional? Do you speak as a professional? Does your business card or brochure look and feel professional?

Dress professionally and wear an outfit with two easily accessible pockets. Make sure you're well groomed and leave the euphemisms, foul language, and dirty jokes at home. If you don't already have a permanent name badge with both your and your company's name, purchase one. Order a badge that's high quality, attractive, and has your name imprinted with letters that are large enough to be easily read.

Your time at the event will be broken into three segments. Greeting at the front door, mingling and meeting as many people as possible, and then seeking out the people you met who are of real interest for a second conversation. Most networking events are 2 to 2½ hours in length. Plan on spending the first 20 minutes greeting people at the door, an hour to an hour and a half mingling, and the last 30 to 45 minutes reconnecting with people who are of real interest to you.

Position yourself close to the main entrance and make every effort to greet each person who enters. Don't spend time engaging in conversation, simply note each person, greet them, and, if possible, remember their names. At this point your goal is to simply meet each attendee face to face and, hopefully, put a name with a face so you can greet them later by name as you mingle.

As the area fills with people and new attendees begin to dwindle, begin your real interaction with fellow attendees. Since you're at the main entrance, begin in one direction and start a conversation with the person closest to you. Greet him or her by name and introduce yourself again (assuming you met him or her as he or she entered). Offer a handshake while asking about his or her business. During this conversation you want to keep the focus on the other person as much as possible. Most people enjoy talking about themselves, and since they're attending a networking event it's fair to assume they're looking to meet people who could be prospects for them. Therefore, their primary interest is in telling people about their business. Accommodate them. Focusing the conversation on the other person allows you to qualify him or her. The more you learn about him or her and his or her business, the better you can make a decision about whether this person is a real prospect.

During the conversation you'll be asked about your business. Use your standard 30- to 40-word infomercial. If you've constructed a good infomercial, you're new acquaintance will ask a follow-up question about what you do. Explain your business briefly and return the topic of the conversation to the other person.

Each initial conversation should be short—2 to 4 minutes. Then, either find another person you can bring into the conversation, or excuse yourself to meet someone else.

At most events you'll notice a number of people who seem to have a difficult time introducing themselves to others. These people will stand off by themselves, usually nursing a drink. The simple act of addressing them and bringing them into your conversation will go a long way in gaining their support. Most of these people find such events awkward. Having someone recognize them and help them begin a conversation is the equivalent of throwing them a life-preserver. They won't forget your kindness. And, who knows? They just might be your next big sale or become your best referral source.

As you meet people, use your pockets to help segregate the business cards you collect. In your left pocket, put the business cards of people you have no interest in pursuing as potential business prospects. In your right pocket, put the business cards of those who interest you. When you segregate the cards as you meet people you don't have to worry about remembering who was of interest as you try and sort through the cards later. It's already done—and soon you'll need those right-pocket business cards.

Continue around the room in this manner for most of the allotted time. As you meet people you have a serious interest in pursuing, let them know you enjoyed the conversation, you hope to see them again before the end of the event, and ask permission to call them later in the week to continue the conversation if you miss them later. You want them to know of your interest and you want their permission— and expectation—that you'll contact them either later in the event or within a few days. Once you have their permission to reconnect, you have reason to believe they also have an interest in continuing the conversation with you. You can call them within a few days with the full expectation that they'll take your call. Before moving to meet another person, take another of your cards or small brochures and use the blank area on the back to handwrite your mobile number and when you will call them—a specific time and date. You'll be placing the cards you get from these people in your right pocket, so make your call time the same for everyone. Using a time such as Thursday between 10:30 and 11:30 gives you an hour to make your calls—and you don't have to re- member who you were supposed to call when. Any card in your right pocket gets a call between 10:30 and 11:30 on Thursday, unless you set a lunch meeting when you met them later in the event.

The last portion of the event, about 30 to 45 minutes, will con- sist of seeking out the best prospects you determined during your ini- tial conversation. Concentrate on finding the people whose cards are in your right pocket. As you locate one, approach as you would greet anyone you know personally—say his or her name, offer a handshake, and inquire what he or she thinks of the event. Assume that he or she remembers you. Now he or she is putting you into his or her mental database as an acquaintance, no longer someone he or she briefly met.

As with your initial conversation, this conversation will also be very short—3 or 4 minutes. The purpose of this conversation is to reinforce your name and face, and possibly set up a lunch meeting. Once you've set a meeting, write your mobile number and the specifics of the meeting time, date, and location on the back of one of your cards or brochures.

It's possible you could've set a meeting date with your first conversation near the door, but you want to delay that until the second meeting with a prospect. Studies show it takes approximately seven interactions with someone before he or she recognizes you as an acquaintance and begins to build trust. By allowing yourself to interact twice with your best prospects during the course of the event, then setting a lunch meeting within a few days of the event, you've moved almost halfway through the getting-acquainted phase. If you can find a reason during the lunch meeting to drop by your prospect's office within a day or two (perhaps to drop off some printed information), you've jumped ahead to the fifth interaction—all within a week of your initial meeting. If any of your prospects have already left the event, you gained their permission during your initial conversation to follow up with them in a couple of days with a phone call.

After the event, send each of the people you met a thank you note for taking time to speak with you. Even those you determined weren't prospects should be accorded that respect; you never know who might send you an occasional referral. The note to your prospects should remind them of the time, date, and location of your lunch meeting. Also immediately add each of these people to your CRM database.

Follow up is one of the most difficult tasks to accomplish. Time is a commodity most salespeople have trouble managing. Setting a specific time to send thank you notes and enter these people into your database on the day after an event will help keep you from losing good prospects. Most of us have met good prospects we ended up wasting because we failed to follow up in a timely manner. Eventually we had to forget about contacting that person, because we were embarrassed at the time lapse between meeting the prospect and our follow up. If you aren't going to work your prospects, why spend the time and effort generating them? Once you identify a quality prospect, act quickly to put that name into your system. As with promises to your clients, keeping your commitments to the people you've just met is essential. If you make a promise to call, you must call. If you get a receptionist or voice mail, leave a message so the prospect knows you called as promised.

By working this method and attending at least three networking events a month, you'll eventually establish a broad base of people who send you business. Each may only send one or two referrals a year, but with enough contacts like this, your sales efforts can be supplemented nicely through working networking events.

CHAPTER **14**

Common Objections to Referral Selling

Following are the most common objections I receive from salespeople who believe they can't (or shouldn't) use referral selling in their business:

1. I'm new to selling and don't have a client base. The beginning of a sales career is the perfect time to incorporate techniques from *Creating a Million-Dollar-a-Year Sales Income* into your business. You don't need a lengthy client list to begin selling by referral; all you need is to learn the techniques and use them. Of course, the better prepared and more experienced you are, the more immediate benefit you'll receive from these techniques. But it's never too early—or too late—to start selling by referral. If you're new to sales, the material in this book will help you jump-start your career.

2. My clients don't know anyone they can refer me to. If many of your clients claim they can't provide referrals, then one of two things must be true: (1) you're selling a very personal and sensitive product or service and the client feels uncomfortable revealing his or her purchase to others, or (2) your clients don't trust you or they question your professionalism. If you're selling a relatively common product, whether to individuals or businesses, then many of your clients know others who need your products or services. If you can't get customers to provide referrals, then you should look at yourself, your company, and your product or service to find out why. When asked properly, people will give referrals—lots of them. They only become reluctant when they're afraid of being embarrassed by the product, the salesman, or the company. If you learn the techniques in this book and perform beyond your clients' expectations, each client will be happy to give quality referrals.

3. I'm a (fill in the blank). I don't sell. Oh, how often I've heard this—especially from salespeople in certain industries, such as financial planners, attorneys, CPAs, other consultants, independent IT contractors, and others who view themselves as professionals above the title of "salesperson." The truth is, we're all salespeople. Everyone is selling something, and we all need to improve our selling careers. Those in the "professional" world should be more anxious than most to learn the techniques of PWWR, since referral selling allows us to adopt a more professional, "above the common salesperson" stance with clients.

4. I get so many referrals I can't use any more: About 15% of salespeople already generate a large number of referrals. If you're in that group, then congratulations! You're obviously doing things the right way and chances are you'll recognize your own business practices in this book.

5. I'm new. It all sounds good, but no one will believe me if I try this stuff. You're right, no one will believe you if you don't believe it yourself. Just because you're new to sales doesn't mean you have to act that way. I've seen people who've been in sales for only a few weeks sell more than men and women in their company who've been in the business for years. If you're new to sales work, take the time, energy, and money to learn everything you can about selling in general and selling your product or service in particular. Then practice until it becomes second nature. There are no rules in selling that say because you're a greenhorn you have to act like one, think like one, or telegraph to the world that you're new. Your learning curve can be as steep and fast as you want. Put in the time and the effort to learn quickly and you'll become a true professional in a short time.

6. I get lots of referrals and most are a waste of time. I find (fill in the blank) works best for me. Many experienced salespeople make this remark because they've found a comfortable way to generate enough new clients to survive. However, I usually don't hear this objection from *successful* salespeople. Successful salespeople are willing to invest time and money to find new and better ways to work their businesses. Those who struggle to stay in business every year are usually the men and women who say the referral generation methods in *Creating a Million-Dollar-a-Year Sales Income* are too hard. Perhaps that's because they're looking for the magic formula for easy sales. (It doesn't exist.) As for the quality of referrals, please see the previous answer to question number 2.

195

7. **I've been selling for X number of years and haven't used any of this stuff. I seem to be getting along just fine. Why should I change what I'm doing?** Again, the argument contained in *Creating a Million-Dollar-a-Year Sales Income* isn't that every salesperson is failing or should change the way he or she does business. If your business generates the volume and income you want, then don't change. On the other hand, if you haven't reached a saturation point, the PWWR Referral Generation System can help boost your business and your bank account. There is a simple reason the megaproducers use these techniques—they work.

8. **My clients are (fill in the blank—physicians, sports stars, Fortune 100 executives, and so on) and they're too busy to give referrals.** This is a self-imposed limitation by salespeople who are afraid to ask for referrals. Many salespeople have received hundreds, even thousands, of high-quality referrals from clients who are typically considered too busy to be bothered. Most of the time, my "too busy" clients are happy to sit with me for 20 or 30 minutes and give me referrals; others are more creative. Some had assistants go over their address book with me, while others had their husband or wife go through the address book and let me pick who I wanted to contact. If you've developed a proper relationship, done a quality job, and communicated the importance of referrals for you (and for them)—busy clients will find a way to give you referrals.

9. **All this seems like a lot of effort for a couple of referrals.** It *is* a lot of work for just a couple of referrals. If your objective is to get two or three referrals from clients, then don't bother to learn and implement the techniques in this book. It isn't worth it. If you want to generate a large number of referrals—that's a completely different story.

10. What a crock! I've had attendees sit through my seminars and then pronounce the whole concept "a crock." They believe no salesperson would go to all this trouble to get referrals, no client would give that many referrals, no one can generate enough referrals to work exclusively from them, and no salesperson can be good enough or organized enough to do everything contained within this method. They're right: For them, it is a crock. If they won't take time to do things correctly, nothing in this book will work. For those who want the easy way out, the PWWR Referral Generation System is a crock. However, if you're a salesperson who wants to generate a large number of referrals—and you're willing to work for it—PWWR will elevate you to a new level of sales and income. The million-dollar-a-year sales superstars didn't get where they are by prospecting—they got there by turning their clients into their sales force. If emulating the megaproducers is a crock, then spending your life knocking on doors and hearing "no" more often than "yes" is your alternative.

INDEX

INDEX